220.1

THE GREAT PARENTHESIS

BOOKS BY DR. H. A. IRONSIDE

The Lamp of Prophecy

Care for God's Fruit Trees

Addresses on the Gospel of John

In the Heavenlies

A Continual Burnt Offering

An Historical Sketch of the Brethren Movement
  etc.

THE GREAT PARENTHESIS

Timely Messages on the Interval
Between the 69th and 70th Weeks of
Daniel's Prophecy

by

H. A. IRONSIDE, D.D., Litt.D
Pastor, Moody Memorial Church, Chicago

SECOND EDITION

ZONDERVAN

ZONDERVAN PUBLISHING HOUSE
GRAND RAPIDS, MICHIGAN

Eight Forty-Seven Ottawa Ave.
Grand Rapids, Michigan

PREFACE

The contents of the present volume are really an enlargement of lectures on Bible prophecy that have been given at various conferences during the past few years. It was never convenient to have these stenographically reported at the time of their delivery, and so the substance of the addresses has been very carefully gone over and is now presented for the consideration of those who are interested in the revelation which the Spirit of God has given concerning things to come. It is the author's fervent conviction that the failure to understand what is revealed in Scripture concerning the Great Parenthesis between Messiah's rejection, with the consequent setting aside of Israel nationally, and the regathering of God's earthly people and recognition by the Lord in the last days, is the fundamental cause for many conflicting and unscriptural prophetic teachings. Once this parenthetical period is understood and the present work of God during this age is apprehended, the whole prophetic program unfolds with amazing clearness.

It is not with any pretension of having discovered something new that I have prepared this volume. I am glad to acknowledge my indebtedness to many sober, spiritually-minded teachers of the Word who in years gone by saw clearly many truths as to God's prophetic plan which later writers and teachers have obscured in large measure. While I do not expect all my readers to agree with me, I humbly ask that, like the Berean Jews of old, they do not reject this testimony without careful inquiry, but that they search the Scriptures to see whether these things are so. Personally, they have been a part of my own thinking for so many years and have meant so much to me in my study of the Word of God that I am eager to have others enter into them, too. On the other hand, I have no desire to press anything that is not substantiated by Scripture. "We can do nothing against the truth, but for the truth." And in the Old Testament it is written: "To the law and to the testimony: if they speak not according to this word, it is because there is no light in them."

H. A. IRONSIDE.

Chicago, Ill.

CONTENTS

CHAPTER I

INTRODUCTION

It is noticeable that every major conflict between nations for many centuries past has resulted in a greatly increased interest in the study of the prophetic Scriptures. When men see everything shaking to pieces which they have supposed to be firm and stable, it is not to be wondered at that they begin to inquire concerning those things which cannot be shaken, as set forth in God's Holy Word. Unfortunately, we are all creatures of limitations, and our thinking and our outlook are very likely to be bounded in great measure by the circumstances of the times in which our lot is cast. Thus there has ever been an inclination on the part of many students of prophecy to try to fit the events of which they themselves have cognizance into the prophetic picture as given in the Word. Ever since the Napoleonic wars, for instance, how many efforts have been made to identify certain outstanding characters as the Beast or the Antichrist, and how often have predictions been confidently made that events going on at a particular time were heading up to Armageddon and would bring within a very few months or years the end of the present age, the return of Christ, and the setting up of His Millennial Kingdom!

It is always right to be watching and waiting for the coming of the Lord. This we are commanded to do. "That blessed hope and the appearing of the glory of

9

our great God and Saviour Jesus Christ" should ever be the lodestar of our souls as we journey on over the sea of life; and surely every instructed Christian, saddened and wearied by man's vain efforts to bring about and insure a lasting peace on earth, must look with eager, glad anticipation to the promised Second Advent of the Prince of Peace, who is to reign in righteousness and bring deliverance to the troubled world.

But time and again prophetic teachers have attempted to work out various systems of chronology drawn partially or wholly from Scripture or in other cases drawn from some fanciful interpretation of the Great Pyramid in Egypt, the stars in their courses, or even the predictions of charlatans like Nostradamus, Mother Shipton and others. Most of these systems prove popular for a time, but as a rule their overconfident exploiters set the dates for the fulfillment of their hopes so close at hand that they themselves live to see their prophecies proved utterly false. Others pass away before their predictions are shown to be wrong, and yet in many instances these attempted efforts to set the time for Messiah's Second Advent are worked over by others and added to in such a way as to modernize them and apply them to new and changed conditions, but all at last are proved to be false.

The reason for this is, as I honestly believe, that we are living in a period concerning which we have absolutely no chronology in the Word of God, and certainly nothing in the Great Pyramid, to guide us. I only refer to the Pyramid because so many have based their faith upon what they fancy to be its corroboration of their theories. I do not for one moment believe it is the predicted altar to be set up at the border of the land of Egypt, for it is not an altar at all, but a great mausoleum. The Word of God needs no outside corroboration. It is complete in itself. "All scripture is given by inspiration of God, and is profitable for doctrine, for reproof, for correction, for instruction in righteousness: that the man of God may be perfect, thoroughly furnished unto all good works." If the Word of God can perfect the man of God completely, then he needs not to add anything to it in order to obtain this desired end.

It is a recognized principle in the ways of God with men to present certain privileges to them or give certain promises which, however, are contingent as to the time of fulfillment upon the faith and obedience of those to whom they are given. Some outstanding promises do not come under these limitations. God's covenant with Abraham was one of pure grace. Nothing that has happened since or can happen will change it in the least degree. Through Abraham's glorious Seed, our Lord Jesus Christ, all nations shall yet be blessed in accordance with the promise. But other promises have been given which were dependent upon faith and obedience for their fulfillment. One has only to think of God's promises to Israel that they should inherit the land of Palestine and possess it in spite of all the efforts of their enemies to dislodge them, provided they walked in obedience to His Holy Word. This they failed to do, and therefore they lost their land, but the same God who told them that this would be the result of their waywardness, has also declared that the time will come when they will return to that land and will become a regenerated nation who will worship the Lord in the beauty of holiness.

It has often been pointed out by others, but is well worth repeating, that the Old Testament seer might be likened to a man standing on one of our Western plains looking off toward a great mountain range. Many miles before him is a vast mountain which for the moment fills all his vision. Clouds cover the top of it, so that it seems to pierce the heavens, but suddenly the clouds are lifted and in the blaze of the westering sun he sees another and higher peak beyond, covered with snow, which seems to shine in resplendent glory. What the man gazing upon this scene cannot see, however, is the valley or the lower ranges of mountains that come in between these two peaks. The one may be many miles beyond the other. In between may be lesser hills, valleys, rivers, villages and farms, but all of these are unseen by the man upon the plain.

Let us imagine a cross surmounting the first peak, and call this the vision of the coming of the Lord Jesus Christ to suffer and to die for our sins. Then imagine that the glory surrounding the second and higher peak takes the form of a crown of light, and think of it as indicating the Second Coming of our Lord Jesus to reign in power and glory over all this lower universe. Peter spoke of the "sufferings of Christ, and the glory that should follow." These two mountains illustrate both. But now, in between them we have all the events of the present age of grace, and these could not be seen by the Old Testament prophets for it was not yet the will of God to make them known. These are the mysteries kept secret from the foundation of the world, which began to be made manifest by our Lord Jesus as He told of the mysteries of the kingdom of heaven; and then were more fully unfolded in the unique revelation of the mystery of the Church, the body of Christ, given to the Apostle Paul, and the unfolding of the mystery of iniquity and of Babylon the Great through Paul and John. Other mysteries there are linked with these, and nearly all of them have to do with what is going on between the First and Second Comings of our Lord.

The chronological periods given in the prophets, otherwise called "the times and the seasons," have to do with God's earthly people Israel, and therefore with events up to the cross when the Lord was rejected, and other events which will not begin to take place so long as the Church is in this scene, for that Church is in itself the unfolding of the mystery which has been hid in God from before the foundation of the world, and is now made manifest for the obedience of faith among all nations.

It is my purpose in these chapters to show that this hidden period of time which has now extended over nineteen centuries was intimated by the Old Testament prophets and has been confirmed in the New Testament, but that through losing sight of it, many have missed the mind of God entirely in regard to the working out of His great plan for the blessing of Israel, the salvation of the nations, and the unique place which the Church as the body of Christ has in the counsels of God, and will have for all eternity. I believe it can be shown from Scripture that this Great Parenthesis is the true key to a right understanding of prophecy. This key once laid hold of will save from much blundering, and certainly should deliver the people of God from discouragement when it almost looks as though God's plans have gone awry and are not working out according to His mind. The fact is, He is working everything according to the counsel of His own will, but many of us have failed to understand what that counsel involves.

With these preliminary thoughts in mind then, shall we go on to examine a number of Scriptures in which the Great Parenthesis is clearly indicated, and as we do so, may God grant that it be in dependence upon His Holy Spirit, to keep us from missing His mind, and to lead us, in accordance with the promise of our Lord, into all truth, as He takes of the things of Christ and shows them to us and makes known unto us things to come.

Chapter II

THE GREAT PROPHECY OF THE SEVENTY WEEKS

We have in the ninth chapter of the book of Daniel the most remarkable time prophecy of the Holy Scriptures. Sir Edward Denny was, I think, perhaps the first prophetic student to designate this chapter, "The Backbone of Prophecy." He may, of course, have borrowed the term from someone else, but if so, the present writer has never found it used by anyone who wrote earlier than this particular teacher. The term is well given, for if we understand the outline indicated here, we shall find that all the prophetic Scriptures fall into place without forcing them, and that so simply as to make it evident that we have here the backbone of the entire prophetic system of the Bible.

Those who have given much study to the book of Daniel will remember that the chapter begins with an account of Daniel's personal exercises. He tells us that he had been studying the books of some of the prophets who had gone before him. He refers to the book of Jeremiah for one (Chap. 29:10-14), and probably the second book of Chronicles (36:21), for another. In these books he learned that God would accomplish seventy years in the desolations of Jerusalem. It had been definitely foretold that following the destruction of the city and Temple and the enslavement of God's earthly people in Babylon, a period of seventy years would elapse ere they would be restored to their own land and be permitted to rebuild the Temple, and eventually the city of Jerusalem itself.

Daniel had been carried away in one of the first of the campaigns against Palestine. He was then but a youth, and now had become an old man. He realized, therefore, that the seventy-year cycle must be nearly completed. This stirred his heart to prayer — which in itself is most suggestive. How often people take up the study of prophecy from a purely intellectual standpoint, and yet surely there is nothing to move our hearts toward God like occupation with His marvelous purpose in regard to the coming of His own blessed Son into the world again and the setting up of His glorious kingdom.

Daniel felt in his soul that the people were not in a fit state for restoration, and he took the place of confession before God. He himself was perhaps one of the holiest men living at that time, and yet, as he prostrates himself before the Lord, he identifies himself with the sins of his people as he cries, "I and my people have sinned." As he pours out his heart in contrition, he counts on God to work deliverance, and in answer to his prayer, a messenger is sent from the Throne of God, even Gabriel himself, the same glorious being who appeared to him on a later occasion, and who at the beginning of New Testament times was chosen to convey to the blessed Virgin Mary the wondrous news that she was to be the destined mother of the promised Messiah.

There is something moving in the way the Spirit of God directs attention to the time when Gabriel first appeared to Daniel. We are told that he "touched him about the time of the evening oblation." That is, it was the time when, if things had been right in Israel, the evening sacrifice would have been offered on the altar at Jerusalem; but that altar was cast down; the Temple was in ruins. No smoke of sacrifice ascended to God from that holy place. Yet Daniel never forgot the time when the oblation should have been placed upon the altar.

Of course, that offering spoke of the sacrifice of our Lord Jesus which was yet to take place. God Himself saw in every victim placed on Jewish altars a type of the Person and work of His own beloved Son; and everything that God will yet accomplish for Israel, for the Church, and for the nations, will be based upon the finished work of Calvary's cross. Our Lord there "tasted death for every man." Actually, the last word is in the neuter in the original. Our Lord tasted death for every *thing*. The blessing of the entire universe is contingent upon the work which He accomplished on the cross.

Now let us note the message or the prophecy that Gabriel brought to Daniel. We read in verses 24 to 27:

> "Seventy weeks are determined upon thy people and upon thy holy city, to finish the transgression, and to make an end of sins, and to make reconciliation for iniquity, and to bring in everlasting righteousness, and to seal up the vision and prophecy, and to anoint the most Holy. Know therefore and understand, that from the going forth of the commandment to restore and to build Jerusalem unto the Messiah the Prince shall be seven weeks, and threescore and two weeks: the street shall be built again, and the wall, even in troublous times. And after threescore and two weeks shall Messiah be cut off, but not for himself:

and the people of the prince that shall come shall
destroy the city and the sanctuary; and the end thereof shall be with a flood, and unto the end of the war
desolations are determined. And he shall confirm the
covenant with many for one week: and in the midst
of the week he shall cause the sacrifice and the
oblation to cease, and for the overspreading of
abominations he shall make it desolate, even until
the consummation, and that determined shall be
poured upon the desolate."

There are a few items here which become a little
clearer if we turn to other translations. For instance, in
verse 25, the latter part, the Revised Version reads: "It
shall be built again, with street and moat, even in troublous times." Some versions read in place of "troublous
times," "the *narrow* times." Then in verse 26, the marginal reading seems better than the received text: "After
the sixty-two weeks shall Messiah be cut off, and shall
have nothing." The latter part of verse 26 is given in
the Revised Version as: "Even unto the end shall be
war; desolations are determined." And in verse 27, the
last half of the verse reads in the Revised Version:
"Upon the wing of abominations shall one come that
maketh desolate." Other slight differences are found in
various versions, but they need not occupy us now.

Let us weigh carefully just what is here revealed.
Remember in the first place, Daniel had understood by
books the number of the years in which God would
accomplish the desolations of Jerusalem. His prayer
of confession is with that in view. God meets him by
informing him through His angel that not at the expiration of seventy years but at the close of seventy weeks
will all Israel's sorrows come to an end. The word

translated *week* is recognized by scholars generally as a generic term simply meaning a *seven*. It could be used for a seven of days, a seven of months, or, as is undoubtedly the case here, a seven of years, since it was of years that Daniel was thinking. Seventy weeks of years, then, would be 490 years.

Now let us observe exactly what the angel says. "Seventy sevens are determined," or "cut off" (that is, cut off from the entire period of time). These seventy seven's, or 490 years, are set apart in the divine reckoning for what the angel calls, "Thy people and thy holy city," that is, Daniel's people, certainly the people of the Jews, and his holy city, Jerusalem, the literal capital of the land of Palestine.

Now, what will take place at the expiration of this period of 490 years? The angel adds: "To finish the transgression, and to make an end of sins, and to make reconciliation [or atonement] for iniquity, and to bring in everlasting righteousness, and to seal up the vision and prophecy, and to anoint the most Holy." Notice carefully each of these expressions. At the end of 490 years, Israel's transgression will be finished, and their sins brought to an end, because their Messiah will have made reconciliation or atonement for iniquity. The long period of Israel's sufferings under the heel of the Gentiles will be completed, and everlasting righteousness will be brought in. This refers clearly to the setting up of Messiah's kingdom. Then the vision and prophecy will be sealed up. That is, all will be fulfilled so that vision and prophecy will no longer be needed; and last of all, the most Holy will be anointed. This must refer,

I believe, to the Shekinah glory returning to Israel when the people are gathered back in their own land and Jehovah's Temple is rebuilt. The glory has been missing ever since the destruction of Jerusalem by Nebuchadnezzar. It was not seen in the temple of Zerubbabel nor in the temple of Herod, but it will return when Israel's mourning shall be ended and, as a repentant people, they will be brought back to God. Thus far, then, the promise of verse twenty-four.

Now, if we can find out just when the 490-year period was to begin, it ought to be an easy thing to count 490 years from that point and then to ask, "Have all these promises been fulfilled?" The starting point is given in the next verse. "Know therefore and understand, that from the going forth of the commandment to restore and to build Jerusalem" — let us stop there for a moment. This is clearly the time from which we are to begin to count. When did a commandment go forth to restore and to build Jerusalem? Right here there is a difference of opinion among sober teachers of prophecy. Some insist that the reference is to the commandment given in the seventh chapter of the book of Ezra, which was approximately 457 B.C.; but a careful examination of that decree will make it evident that it did not really have to do with restoring and building the city of Jerusalem at all, but was rather a confirmation of the earlier decree of Cyrus to rebuild the Temple and reinstate the worship of God in Israel. It seems far more likely that the commandment referred to is actually that given in the second chapter of the book of Nehemiah. There we have in very truth a commandment to restore and build

Jerusalem, and that commandment was given about 445 B.C.

We are not told whether the sevens of years are to be counted according to sun time or lunar time, and for our present purpose it is not necessary that we should go into the problem here. Sir Robert Anderson, in his masterly work, *The Coming Prince,* has taken it up in great detail, and has presented a chronological system which seems fully satisfactory, though all are not prepared to accept it. Those who are interested may consult that work at their leisure. I shall not deal with chronology as such here. I only desire to emphasize that evidently we have in Nehemiah 2 the starting point for this time prophecy.

But now let us go on with the quotation of the rest of the verse: "From the going forth of the commandment to restore and to build Jerusalem unto the Messiah the Prince shall be seven weeks, and threescore and two weeks." Here, then, we have sixty-nine weeks — not seventy. In other words, 483 years — not 490. For some reason the angel separates the last week of seven years from the sixty-nine which were to be completed at the coming of Messiah the Prince. And these sixty-nine weeks are divided into two periods — seven weeks, or forty-nine years, and sixty-two weeks, or 434 years. Undoubtedly the division here is in order to prepare our minds for a further division between the sixty-ninth and the seventieth weeks.

We are told: "The street shall be built again, and the wall, even in troublous times," or, as other translations read, "in the narrow," or "the straitened times." The reference is evidently to the seven weeks as distinguished from the threescore and two weeks. The former period is called "the narrow times," and during those forty-nine years the city of Jerusalem was rebuilt and the people gathered back to it. They were troublous times in measure, but the reference is evidently not so much to the distress of the people at that time as to the fact that the city was built in the narrow period.

The sixty-two weeks begin immediately after the expiration of the seven weeks, and we are told in verse 26: "And after threescore and two weeks shall Messiah be cut off and have nothing." If Sir Robert Anderson be correct in his system of chronology, this tremendous event occurred within a literal week after the exact close of the sixty-nine weeks of years. He points out that sixty-nine years of 360 days each, expired when our Lord was welcomed into Jerusalem by the children and others who cried, "Hosannah; Blessed is he that cometh in the name of the Lord." However, we are not told that Messiah would be cut off at the exact time of the expiration of the sixty-two weeks, but "*after* threescore and two weeks shall Messiah be cut off." This part of the prophecy has been fulfilled to the letter. "He came unto his own, and his own received him not." He presented Himself to Israel as their promised King-Messiah. They said, "We will not have this man to reign over us," and demanded that He be crucified. Pilate asked, "Shall I crucify your King?" They exclaimed, "We have no king but Caesar." And so the Messiah for whom the nation had waited so long was crucified. Following that, if we are to take the seventieth week as an immediate continuation of the period which ended at the cross, in seven years from the time of the Saviour's crucifixion all the promises made to Israel should have been fulfilled!

The fact is, they were not fulfilled. Israel did not recognize their Messiah. They do not know Him yet as their Sinbearer. Their transgression has not been finished. An end of sins for them has not been made. They do not know anything yet of atonement for iniquity. Everlasting righteousness has not been brought in. Vision and prophecy have not been sealed up. The most Holy has not been anointed by the return of the Shekinah. What then? Has the prophecy failed? Has God's Word been proved to be false? Impossible! We know that He cannot deny Himself. But it is right here that we find one of the great and important truths of the Word.

Between the sixty-ninth and the seventieth weeks we have a Great Parenthesis which has now lasted over nineteen hundred years. The seventieth week has been postponed by God Himself who changes the times and the seasons because of the transgression of the people. As I have put it elsewhere, though some have objected to the expression, the moment Messiah died on the cross, the prophetic clock stopped. There has not been a tick upon that clock for nineteen centuries. It will not begin to go again until the entire present age has come to an end, and Israel will once more be taken up by God.

Let us turn again to the prophecy and see definitely what is there predicted. After the declaration to Daniel that Messiah would be cut off and have nothing after the conclusion of the 483-year period, we read: "And the people of the prince that shall come shall destroy the city and the sanctuary; and the end thereof shall be with a flood, and unto the end wars and desolations are determined." Now what exactly is it that is here predicted? Messiah was cut off. He had nothing so far as the kingdom so long promised and expected was concerned. Shortly after His crucifixion, the Roman people came and destroyed the city and the Sanctuary. We are not told just when this would take place. Actually, it was forty years after. Also observe that it is not said here that the prince would come and destroy the city. A prince is in view who is yet to play a large part in prophecy. He, however, has not appeared yet, but his people, that is, the Roman people, were used as the scourge of God to punish Israel for their sins, and they destroyed Jerusalem and the Temple of Jehovah.

Then we have all the present age put into three lines: "The end thereof shall be with a flood, and unto the end wars and desolations are determined." That is, as by an overflowing flood the people of Israel were to be destroyed by their enemies, scattered throughout the world, and until the end, that is, the seventieth week, which remains unfulfilled, there shall be wars and desolations. This is exactly what our Saviour Himself tells us, as recorded in Matthew 24. During all the present age, "ye shall hear of wars and rumors of wars: see that ye be not troubled: for all these things must come to pass, but the end is not yet." That end is again the seventieth week.

Throughout the book of Daniel we have the expression frequently, "the time of the end." The same expression is found elsewhere in the prophetic Scriptures. The time of the end is the last seven years of the times which God has allotted to the people of the Jews, which has not yet begun to run its course. We shall see as we continue our studies what God is doing in this intervening period which we have designated, "The Great Parenthesis."

When this time of waiting comes to an end, then the prince whose people have already appeared shall himself appear; that is, the great Roman leader of the last days, called in Revelation 13, "the Beast" because he is emphatically the embodiment of every evil principle in all the empires of the world. When he appears, he will pretend at first to be the friend of the Jews, and we read in verse 27: "He shall confirm the covenant with many for one week: and in the midst of the week he shall cause the sacrifice and the oblation to cease, and for the overspreading of abominations he shall make it desolate, even until the consummation, and that determined shall be poured upon the desolate," or, as some read, "the desolator." Strange is it that many have supposed it was Prince Messiah Himself who was to confirm a covenant for one week. But when did He ever make such a covenant? The blood of the covenant which He shed upon the cross is not to confirm a covenant for seven years, but it is the blood of the everlasting covenant.

In the last days when God takes Israel up again and is about to bring them into fullness of blessing, a Roman prince will arise who will make a covenant with the nation for seven years, promising them protection and liberty in religion as they return to their land. For three and one-half years he will permit this to go on, but in the midst of the week he will violate the covenant and demand that all worship to Jehovah cease, and the Antichrist will be manifested in his true character. This will result in what is known in Scripture as the time of Jacob's trouble, or the Great Tribulation, and it will go on for three and one-half years until judgment is visited upon the desolator, and God's earthly people are delivered. The greater part of the book of the Revelation, in fact virtually everything from chapter four to the end of chapter nineteen, has to do with events which will take place in heaven and on earth during this last unfulfilled seventieth week of Daniel. When this is seen, all is wonderful harmony, and the prophetic Scriptures are plain.

CHAPTER III

THE ACCEPTABLE YEAR OF THE LORD

When once the break in the prophetic plan is seen as set forth in Daniel 9, one recognizes the fact that provision is made for this in prophetic interpretation throughout the entire Word of God. Prophecy has to do first with events connected with the nations in contact with Israel before and up to the coming of and rejection of the Messiah. Then there is a long interval during which, we learn from the New Testament, God is doing a work never mentioned in Old Testament times. Following this we have prophecies relating to the coming judgments at the time of the end and the Second Advent in power and glory of our Lord as He takes possession of the kingdom so long predicted.

A very striking instance is that of Isaiah 61; of which a portion was read and commented on by our Saviour at His first return visit to Nazareth, where he had been reared, after His baptism by John and the temptation in the wilderness. We are told by Luke that when He went into the synagogue on the Sabbath Day, and stood up to read, there was delivered unto Him the book of the Prophet Esaias, and when He had opened the book, He found the place where it is written:

"The Spirit of the Lord is upon me, because he hath anointed me to preach the gospel to the poor; he hath sent me to heal the brokenhearted, to preach deliverance to the captives, and recovering of sight

to the blind, to set at liberty them that are bruised,
to preach the acceptable year of the Lord" (Luke
4:16-19).

In the opening words of the next verse we read: "And
he closed the book, and he gave it again to the minister,
and sat down." There is something here that is very
significant. By turning back to Isaiah 61, we find that
He finished reading at a comma, for there in verse 2 we
read:

> "To proclaim the acceptable year of the Lord,
> and the day of vengeance of our God; to comfort all
> that mourn; to appoint unto them that mourn in
> Zion, to give unto them beauty for ashes, the oil of
> joy for mourning, the garment of praise for the
> spirit of heaviness; that they might be called trees
> of righteousness, the planting of the Lord, that he
> might be glorified" (Isaiah 61:2-3).

The remainder of the chapter speaks of the wonderful
blessing which will come to the land of Palestine and
the people of Israel in the last days.

Now when our Lord ceased reading in the middle of
verse 2, He evidently had a very definite reason for it,
and that reason is closely linked with what we have
already been considering in our study of the great prophecy of the seventy weeks. One might suppose, if he had
never considered the matter before, that the entire
prophecy of Isaiah 61 would be continuous. There is
nothing in this Old Testament passage to indicate otherwise; but by closing the book when He did, our Lord
distinguished very definitely between His ministry connected with His First Coming and that which is to take
place when He comes the second time. He ceased read-

ing as He uttered the words, "To proclaim the acceptable year of the Lord." This introduced the Gospel Era. He did not read further because the day of vengeance of our God was not due to begin at that time, and, in fact, it has not yet begun.

In other words, our Lord put the entire dispensation of the grace of God in which we live into a comma. That comma represents a period of nearly two thousand years, at least. How much more, we cannot say. Not one other part of the prophecy has been fulfilled since the Lord closed the book. When Daniel's last seventieth week begins, then the fulfillment of the rest of the prophecy will start, and soon every promise to the people of Israel will be confirmed.

The Lord Jesus came in lowly grace, preaching good tidings unto the meek. He came binding up the broken-hearted, proclaiming liberty to captives and the opening of prison to those who were bound. He preached the acceptable year of the Lord, but Israel rejected Him. They did not recognize in the lowly Nazarene the King whom they were expecting, and so they fulfilled other Scriptures in rejecting Him.

This left God free, if I may put it that way, to open up secrets that had been in His heart from before the foundation of the world, and so we have the glorious age of grace in which we live, the calling out of the Church from Jew and Gentile to be the body and bride of Christ, and to share His throne with Him in the coming age. During all this time Israel nationally is rejected. It is folly to maintain, as some do, that the British nation and kindred peoples are really Israel and that a distinction is now to be made between Israel and the Jews. Before the Assyrian and Babylonian captivities, God made this distinction, but since that time we find the terms "Jew" and "Israelite" used interchangeably. This will be seen clearly when we come to consider the great parenthetical portion of the Epistle to the Romans, chapters 9 to 11. During all this time Israel nationally is set to one side. They are "lost," as it were, among the Gentiles. Individual Israelites may be saved by grace in the same way as individual Gentiles, but God is not dealing with the chosen nation as such.

When this age comes to an end and the Church of God has been caught away to be with the Lord, then will follow the awful period of judgment so frequently referred to in the prophetic Scriptures, "the day of vengeance of our God." It will be the day when God will deal in judgment with apostate Christendom and apostate Judaism, when the vials of his wrath will be poured out upon the guilty nations who have rejected His Word, rejected His Son, and blasphemed His Holy Spirit. That day of vengeance is referred to again and again in the Scriptures under various names. It is called "the great and dreadful day of the Lord," "the time of Jacob's trouble," "the great tribulation," "the coming hour of temptation," and various other terms are also applied to it. It has nothing to do with the trials and tribulations through which the Church of God is now passing. For the Church, the entire period of her testimony here on earth is one of tribulation, even as our Lord said: "In the world ye shall have tribulation, but in me ye shall have peace." And the Apostle Paul tells us: "Ye must through much tribulation enter the kingdom of God." But this is to be distinguished from what is emphatically called *the Great Tribulation*, which takes place after the Rapture of the Church and is the time when God will deal in wrath with the guilty nations of the world.

However, following this day of vengeance comes the time when the Lord will comfort all that mourn. He will return in power to Israel, and the remainder of this sixty-first chapter of Isaiah will have its glorious fulfillment. Note what is predicted in verses 3 to 7. In that day Zion's mourning will be turned to joy; for the ashes of her blighted hopes will be given the beauty of acceptance with God. She will exchange the spirit of heaviness for the garment of praise, and restored Israel will be called "trees of righteousness, the planting of the Lord"; and all this that He might be glorified.

Then will come the blessing of the land, when God's promise to Abraham that the land should be his and in possession of his seed forever, will be literally fulfilled. "And they shall build the old wastes, they shall raise up the former desolations, they shall repair the waste cities, and the desolations of many generations shall come to an end."

Israel will no longer be despised and hated by the nations. The Jew will not be looked upon with contempt and disapproval. Strangers from among the Gentiles, sons of the alien, will delight to serve God's ancient people who themselves will be named the priests of the Lord, and will be recognized as the ministers of our God. Because of all the anguish and wretchedness they have endured throughout the centuries, they will receive in return of the riches of the Gentiles, and will grow in the favor God shall put upon them. Verse 7 is very significant. God will make up to them in a marvelous way for all that they have endured throughout the years of their wanderings, and this in their own land, where everlasting joy shall be upon their heads.

It will be at that time that the promise given through Jeremiah will be fulfilled. In the thirty-first chapter of his prophecy, we have a corroborative passage that is linked definitely with this passage in Isaiah.

> "The Lord hath appeared of old unto me, saying, Yea, I have loved thee with an everlasting love: therefore with lovingkindness have I drawn thee. Again I will build thee, and thou shalt be built, O virgin of Israel: thou shalt again be adorned with thy tabrets, and shalt go forth in the dances of them that make merry. Thou shalt yet plant vines upon the mountains of Samaria: the planters shall plant, and shall eat them as common things. For there shall be a day, that the watchmen upon the mount Ephraim shall cry, Arise ye, and let us go up to Zion unto the Lord our God. For thus saith the Lord; Sing with gladness for Jacob, and shout among the chief of the nations: publish ye, praise ye, and say, O Lord, save thy people, the remnant of Israel. Behold, I will bring them from the north country, and gather them from the coasts of the earth, and with them the blind and the lame, the woman with child and her that travaileth with child together: a great company shall return thither. They shall come with weeping, and with supplications will I lead them: I will cause them to walk by the rivers of waters in a straight way, wherein they shall not stumble: for I am a father to Israel, and Ephraim is my firstborn. Hear the word of the Lord, O ye nations, and declare it in the isles afar off. and say, He that scattered Israel will gather him, and keep

him, as a shepherd doth his flock. For the Lord hath
redeemed Jacob, and ransomed him from the hand
of him that was stronger than he. Therefore they
shall come and sing in the height of Zion, and shall
flow together to the goodness of the Lord, for wheat,
and for wine, and for oil, and for the young of the
flock and of the herd: and their soul shall be as a
watered garden; and they shall not sorrow any more
at all. Then shall the virgin rejoice in the dance,
both young men and old together: for I will turn
their mourning into joy, and will comfort them, and
make them rejoice from their sorrow. And I will
satiate the soul of the priests with fatness, and my
people shall be satisfied with my goodness, saith the
Lord" (Jeremiah 31:3-14).

Then the new covenant will be confirmed with the
house of Israel and with the house of Judah according
to the promise of verses 31 through 34:

"Behold, the days come, saith the Lord, that I will
make a new covenant with the house of Israel, and
with the house of Judah: not according to the covenant that I made with their fathers in the day that
I took them by the hand to bring them out of the
land of Egypt; which my covenant they brake; although I was an husband unto them, saith the Lord:
but this shall be the covenant that I will make with
the house of Israel; After those days, saith the Lord,
I will put my law in their inward parts, and write it
in their hearts; and will be their God, and they shall
be my people. And they shall teach no more every
man his neighbour, and every man his brother, saying, Know the Lord: for they shall all know me,
from the least of them unto the greatest of them, saith
the Lord: for I will forgive their iniquity, and I will
remember their sin no more" (Jeremiah 31:31-34).

This is the covenant referred to in the eighth verse of
Isaiah 61, where God says: "I will direct their work in

truth, and I will make an everlasting covenant with them." The closing verses of the chapter set forth the delight that God will have in His people in that day:

> "And their seed shall be known among the Gen-
> tiles, and their offspring among the people: all that
> see them shall acknowledge them, that they are the
> seed which the Lord hath blessed. I will greatly
> rejoice in the Lord, my soul shall be joyful in my
> God; for he hath clothed me with the garments of
> salvation, he hath covered me with the robe of
> righteousness, as a bridegroom decketh himself with
> ornaments, and as a bride adorneth herself with
> her jewels. For as the earth bringeth forth her bud,
> and as the garden causeth the things that are sown
> in it to spring forth; so the Lord God will cause
> righteousness and praise to spring forth before all
> the nations" (Isaiah 61:9-11).

Let us suppose that we were living in Old Testament times before the First Coming of our Lord Jesus to the earth, and that we were earnest students of the prophetic Word. Imagine, for instance, that we were puzzling over this wonderful portion of Isaiah's prophecy. Could we, by any possibility, realize through reading it that there was a great parenthesis between the two clauses, "the acceptable year of our Lord," and "the day of vengeance of our God"? Daniel 9 is the key that unlocks the truth here as elsewhere, but this was not known at the time that Isaiah wrote. Therefore, we are told in the First Epistle of Peter, chapter 1, that the Old Testament prophets wrote of the coming of Christ, but were utterly unable to understand the times and the seasons connected with this glorious truth. Peter writes:

"Of which salvation the prophets have inquired and searched diligently, who prophesied of the grace that should come unto you: searching what, or what manner of time the Spirit of Christ which was in them did signify, when it testified beforehand the sufferings of Christ, and the glory that should follow. Unto whom it was revealed, that not unto themselves, but unto us they did minister the things, which are now reported unto you by them that have preached the gospel unto you with the Holy Ghost sent down from heaven; which things the angels desire to look into" (I Peter 1:10-12).

In other words, these Old Testament prophets wrote as they were borne along by the Spirit of God, and then, after putting pen to papyrus, they sat down and studied their own writings, pondering them thoughtfully, wondering just what all these marvelous promises could mean, and when they would be fulfilled. They wrote, as Peter again tells us, of the sufferings of Christ and the glories that should follow, but of the interval between the two they knew nothing.

The strange thing is that many Christians ignore it today, and by failing to recognize the importance of this Great Parenthesis, they are in continual perplexity as to the time when prophecy is to be fulfilled.

Chapter IV

FURTHER INSTANCES OF THE HIDDEN INTERVAL

It is not alone in one or two outstanding passages that we find the evidence of the hidden interval between the rejection of Christ and His Second advent, but when once we have recognized the break between the sixty-ninth and seventieth weeks in the time prophecy of Daniel 9, we discern the same thing in passage after passage. In this present chapter it is not my intention to go into any great detail in regard to these, but to point out a number of instances which we shall see, I believe, harmonize perfectly with what has already come before us.

Let us look again at the book of Daniel itself. Throughout that book a period is brought before us called "the time of the end," or "the latter times." When we once get the key to the meaning of this in chapter 9, then everything dovetails perfectly with what is there brought before us. In chapters 2 and 7 we have marvelous visions giving us outlines of the entire period which our Lord designated as "the times of the Gentiles." This expression covers all the years during which Israel and Palestine are under Gentile domination. The Lord said: "Jerusalem shall be trodden down of the Gentiles, until the times of the Gentiles be fulfilled." The expression "trodden down" does not necessarily imply rigorous rule or persecution, but simply that the Gentiles will be in the place of authority. This began with Nebuchadnezzar, and will continue until our Lord returns in triumph and the kingdoms of this world become the kingdom of our God and His Christ.

In Daniel 2 we have "the times of the Gentiles" represented by a great, heroic, human figure composed of gold, silver, brass, iron and clay. The four great world empires, three of which had passed away before Christ came, and the last of which was then in existence, are clearly Babylon, the head of gold; Media-Persia, the breast and arms of silver; Graeco-Macedonia, the body and thighs of brass; and Rome, the legs of iron. The last condition, however, of "the times of the Gentiles," is symbolized by the feet with ten toes, part of iron and part of miry clay or brittle pottery. It is very evident that this last condition has not yet been fully developed. It, therefore, belongs to the time of the end, and will not come into actual existence until the Church of the present age has been caught away to be with the Lord. Then there shall arise ten kingdoms on the basis of the old Roman Empire, which will form an alliance, offensive and defensive; and the prophecy says: "In the days of these kings shall the God of heaven set up a kingdom, which shall never be destroyed."

This is seen even more clearly in the seventh chapter. There, when a man of God has a vision of "the times of the Gentiles," he sees the nations as four great, ravenous beasts, so terrible that there is nothing on earth exactly like them. The last of these beasts represents, like the iron in the image, the Roman Empire, but the final condition of that empire is pictured by ten horns which, of course, correspond to the ten toes on the image.

A careful consideration of verses 23 to 27 will make this clear:

> "Thus he said, The fourth beast shall be the fourth kingdom upon earth, which shall be diverse from all kingdoms, and shall devour the whole earth, and shall tread it down, and break it in pieces. And the ten horns out of this kingdom are ten kings that shall arise: and another shall rise after them; and he shall be diverse from the first, and he shall subdue three kings. And he shall speak great words against the most High, and shall wear out the saints of the most High, and think to change times and laws: and they shall be given into his hand until a time and times and the dividing of time. But the judgment shall sit, and they shall take away his dominion, to consume and to destroy it unto the end. And the kingdom and dominion, and the greatness of the kingdom under the whole heaven, shall be given to the people of the saints of the most High, whose kingdom is an everlasting kingdom, and all dominions shall serve and obey him" (Daniel 7:23-27).

Notice that the Great Parenthesis occurs between verse 23, which pictures to us the Roman Empire as it was in the past, and verse 24, in which we have its final condition. The ten horns we are told are ten kings that shall arise. I will not go into detail here as to the conflict among the kings, resulting in the subjugation of three and the coming to the front of one who will have international authority and think to change times and laws, but I would simply emphasize the fact that this is in full accord with what we find elsewhere in Scripture, as to the manifestation of the last great Gentile ruler who will defy God Himself and seek to destroy everything that is of God in the earth, but when the judgment falls, his dominion will be taken away and then the long promised kingdom of righteousness will be set up under the whole heaven and shall be given to the people of the saints of the most High. This is a remarkable expression. It does not say it shall be given to *the saints of the most High.* The saints of the most High would be those in the heavens, but *the people of the saints of the most High* will be Israel here on earth. They shall enter into and enjoy the kingdom, for all dominions shall serve and obey Christ. Notice that the prophecy does not give us any inkling of what will take place between the rise of the fourth beast and the appearance of the ten horns. All that is included in the present age, and was unseen by prophetic eyes in Old Testament times.

This is corroborated again in chapter 8, which is largely occupied with the conflicts between Persia and Greece, but down to verse 22 we have fulfilled prophecy. Beginning with verse 23 we are carried on to the latter time of the Grecian kingdom when the transgressors are come to the full and "a king of fierce countenance, and understanding dark sentences, shall stand up." This is the last king of the north, who will be the bitter enemy of the people of Israel in the last days, and will vie with the Roman leader in attempting to dominate the land of Palestine. We are told of his activities in verses 24 and 25:

> "And his power shall be mighty, but not by his own power: and he shall destroy wonderfully, and shall prosper, and practise, and shall destroy the mighty and the holy people. And through his policy also he shall cause craft to prosper in his hand; and he shall magnify himself in his heart, and by peace shall destroy many: he shall also stand up against

the Prince of princes; but he shall be broken without hand" (Daniel 8:24-25).

I have gone into this prophecy in my book, *Lectures on the Book of Daniel*, but what I want my readers to see now is that the Great Parenthesis occurs in between verses 22 and 23. All the long period between the last state of the Grecian Empire and the latter times is passed over in silence; yet what momentous events have taken place in those centuries which have already gone!

In chapter 11 we again see the same remarkable prophetic structure. Down to verse 35 we have a marvelous outline of that which has long since been fulfilled in history — the wars between the Seleucidae and Ptolemies, culminating in the resistance and victory of the Maccabees with the assistance of the ships of Chittim, bringing the Roman legions to support the Jewish nationalists. The moral conditions prevailing for a century or more afterwards are given to us in verses 32 to 35, the last verse reading as follows:

> "And some of them of understanding shall fall, to try them, and to purge, and to make them white, even to the time of the end: because it is yet for a time appointed" (Daniel 11:35).

That is, Israel will suffer under Gentile domination until their miseries will be brought to a head and to a conclusion in the time of the end.

The entire present dispensation comes in between verses 35 and 36, the thirty-sixth verse introducing immediately the willful king, the Antichrist of the last days, who will do according to his own will, and exalt himself, and magnify himself above every god, and speak marvelous things against the God of gods, and prosper until the indignation be accomplished, that is, until the vials of the wrath of God have all been poured out upon the earth. The remainder of the chapter has to do with events which will be fulfilled in the last half of the seventieth week of chapter 9, and when we pass into chapter 12, we have the Great Tribulation in all its intensity, followed by Israel's awakening and reward in the Kingdom Age.

The book of Hosea contains moral instruction for the people of Israel designed to awaken them to a recognition of their sad departure from God, so that in the main it does not deal with future events. But there are some remarkable passages in this little book in which we find the same structure that we have been considering. In the earlier verses of chapter 3 we have Jehovah's love for Israel and her unfaithfulness. Then verse 4 is really a description of her condition throughout the entire present parenthetic age. We read:

> "For the children of Israel shall abide many days without a king, and without a prince, and without a sacrifice, and without an image, and without an ephod, and without teraphim" (Hosea 3:4).

We have no details here as to the great historical events that would take place during the long period of Israel's rejection by God following their rejection of Messiah, but in a few graphic sentences we note the things of which they would be deprived.

Verse 5 carries us into the last days:

> "Afterward" (that is, after the long parenthetic period during which they are wandering among the

> nations) "shall the children of Israel return, and
> seek the Lord their God, and David their king; and
> shall fear the Lord and his goodness in the latter
> days" (Hosea 3:5).

The parenthetic interval is found again between the
last verse of chapter 5 and the first verse of chapter 6.
In verse 15 of chapter 5 we hear Messiah Himself speaking, after His own people have refused to recognize Him.
He says:

> "I will go and return to my place, till they acknowl-
> edge their offense, and seek my face: in their afflic-
> tion they will seek me early" (Hosea 5:15).

The first part of this verse was fulfilled literally when
the Lord Jesus ascended to heaven. There He has taken
His place at the Father's right hand, and He waits until
Israel will be brought to recognize their sins and to call
upon Him in repentance. But nearly two thousand years
have passed since our Lord returned to the Father's
house. Meantime Israel remains an unbelieving generation, as the Lord Himself predicted they would, but as
soon as the present interval has passed and the Church
of God has been caught up to be with the Lord, they
themselves will begin to fulfill the opening verses of
chapter 6:

> "Come, and let us return unto the Lord: for he
> hath torn, and he will heal us; he hath smitten, and
> he will bind us up. After two days will he revive us:
> in the third day he will raise us up, and we shall live
> in his sight. Then shall we know, if we follow on
> to know the Lord: his going forth is prepared as the
> morning; and he shall come unto us as the rain, as
> the latter and former rain unto the earth" (Hosea
> 6:1-3).

This will be the day of Israel's repentance. If we remember Peter's words that one day is with the Lord as a thousand years and a thousand years as one day, there may be something more significant in the expressions used in verse 2 than some of us have realized. I do not for a moment favor any date-setting system, and yet one may well raise the question as to whether the two days of that verse might not have reference to the two thousand years of Israel's rejection, and the third day speak of the thousand years of Christ's reign in righteousness.

When we turn to the book of Psalms, we find many similar passages setting forth in juxtaposition the sufferings of Christ and the glories that shall follow. To attempt to point them all out would mean to write a book on the Messianic Psalms, but I would draw attention here to several of them, and the thoughtful reader who searches the Scriptures in dependence upon the Spirit of God will have no difficulty in finding many more.

Psalm 22 has well been called "the Psalm of the Cross" or "the Psalm of the Sin Offering." It begins with our Lord's cry of abandonment: "My God, my God, why hast thou forsaken me?" It ends, if the last words are literally translated, in a cry of triumph: "It is finished." In verses 1 to 21 we have our Lord's sufferings on the cross. Verse 22 tells of His resurrection and His appearance among His own. The Great Parenthesis occurs between verses 22 and 23, for throughout the remainder of the Psalm we have set forth the coming of the kingdom and the deliverance of Israel, based upon that which our Lord endured in His hours of anguish on the tree.

Psalm 110 is frequently referred to in the New Testament, and is recognized by all instructed readers as being definitely Messianic. In the first verse we see our risen, glorified Lord taking His place at the right hand of God. Then comes the prophetic interval for which we have been looking, and following that from verse 2 to the end of the Psalm we have the return of the Lord in power and the establishment of His kingdom on Mount Zion.

I take time to refer to only one other Psalm, and that because of the striking way in which it is used by the Apostle Peter in the New Testament. In I Peter 3:10-12, the Apostle quotes from Psalm 34:12-16:

> "For he that will love life, and see good days, let him refrain his tongue from evil, and his lips that they speak no guile: let him eschew evil, and do good; let him seek peace, and ensue it. For the eyes of the Lord are over the righteous, and his ears are open unto their prayers: but the face of the Lord is against them that do evil" (I Peter 3:10-12).

Now observe how Peter ends his quotation. He says: "The face of the Lord is against them that do evil." Just as Christ Himself stopped reading from Isaiah 61 at a comma, so does the Apostle here, for when we turn back to Psalm 34 we find the complete statement reads: "The face of the Lord is against them that do evil, to cut off the remembrance of them from the earth" (Psalm 34:16). Why did Peter stop in the middle of the sentence? Because, guided by the Holy Spirit, he recognized that the time had not yet come for God to cut off the wicked in judgment from the earth. In other words, he left room for the present age of the times of the

Gentiles to come in between the two parts of the last half of this verse.

To these instances might be added, as I have already intimated, many others; but I trust that these are sufficient to prove the point I am trying to make, namely, that the prophetic Scriptures cannot be understood properly unless this parenthetic period is taken into account, but when once it is seen and recognized as the divine order in God's revelation to mankind, all becomes luminously clear.

CHAPTER V

OUR LORD'S GREAT PROPHECY

In the light of what we have been considering, let us turn now to our Lord's great prophecy uttered on the Mount of Olives shortly before His crucifixion. We find this prophecy recorded in the three Synoptics, namely, in Matthew 24, Mark 13, and Luke 21. It will help us to understand these words aright if we remember that they were uttered just as the sixty-ninth week of Daniel 9 had come to a close. As yet the disciples knew nothing of the long interval that was to elapse ere the seventieth week would be fulfilled. They had already understood to some extent, and yet very feebly, that their Master was about to suffer and to die, but not until after His resurrection did they really comprehend what He meant when He told them that the Son of Man was to be crucified and the third day rise again. They were in the position of a godly Jewish remnant waiting expectantly for the manifestation of the kingdom. They had this and this only in mind when they asked the question: "Tell us, when shall these things be? and what shall be the sign of thy coming, and of the end of the age?"

I take it that most of my readers are well aware of the fact that the expression, "end of the world," as given in the Authorized Version is somewhat misleading. The marginal reading is correct. The end of the age, they knew, would be at the close of the seventieth week, and they were asking the Lord definitely how they might know when that time was about to expire. This is corroborated when we turn to Acts 1, and find these same disciples inquiring of the risen Lord: "Wilt thou at this time restore again the kingdom to Israel?" All their expectations were centered in that kingdom. They knew nothing of the present interval which we speak of as "the dispensation of the grace of God." The mystery of the Church, the one body, had not yet been revealed. Though our Lord had spoken on two occasions of the Church, as recorded in Matthew 16 and again in chapter 18, it is evident that this did not mean to them anything more than the congregation of the righteous. The full revelation of what was in the Lord's mind was to be given later.

In answer to their question, the Saviour did not reprove them because they interpreted Old Testament prophecies literally and looked for an earthly kingdom to be set up at the end of the age, but He told them: "It is not for you to know the times and the seasons which the Father hath put in his own power. But ye shall receive power, after that the Holy Ghost is come upon you, and ye shall be witnesses unto me both in Jerusalem and in all Judaea, and in Samaria and unto the uttermost parts of the earth." What all this implied they did not at first understand. Doubtless He explained many things to them during the forty days between His resurrection and His ascension, as intimated in Acts 1:2-3, but His program for this age was unfolded little by little until the full revelation of the dispensation of the mystery of the one body was given to the Apostle Paul and through him imparted to others.

So then, as we consider Matthew 24, we should try
to put ourselves in the place in which the Apostles were
at that time in order that we may get their mental attitude and understand what it was concerning which they
asked Him; then we shall understand His answer.

He knew that Israel's day was over for that time. He
had already said to them, "Your house is left unto you
desolate." When the disciples looked admiringly upon
the great buildings of the Temple and its surroundings
and exclaimed, "Master, see what great buildings are
here," He replied, "There shall not be left here one stone
upon another, that shall not be thrown down." This must
have amazed them, for they doubtless supposed that in
a very little while He would proclaim Himself as King-
Messiah and that that very Temple would be the center
of Jehovah's worship when the King should reign in
Zion.

And so they asked in surprise for information regarding three things. First, "Tell us, when shall these things
be?" that is, "When will Jerusalem be destroyed? When
will the Temple be thrown down?" We do not get the
answer to that in Matthew 24. When we turn to Luke
21, verses 20 to 24, we find that question fully answered.
Christ's words are as follows:

> "And when ye shall see Jerusalem compassed with
> armies, then know that the desolation thereof is nigh.
> Then let them which are in Judaea flee to the moun-
> tains; and let them which are in the midst of it depart
> out; and let not them that are in the countries enter
> thereinto. For these be the days of vengeance, that
> all things which are written may be fulfilled. But
> woe unto them that are with child, and to them that
> give suck, in those days: for there shall be great dis-

tress in the land, and wrath upon this people. And
they shall fall by the edge of the sword, and shall be
led away captive into all nations: and Jerusalem
shall be trodden down of the Gentiles, until the times
of the Gentiles be fulfilled" (Luke 21:20-24).

The second and the third questions are intimately
linked together. The disciples inquired, "What shall be
the sign of thy coming, and of the end of the age?"
They rightly linked Messiah's manifested presence in
and to Israel with the end of the age. It is this double
question that the Lord answers in the words recorded
in Matthew 24 and in the last part of Luke 21, as also
in Mark 13. In other words, let us bear in mind that
our Lord was not giving His apostles an outline picture
of what would take place during the past nearly two
thousand years, the great interval between His First and
Second Comings. He was speaking to them as to a Jewish remnant who were waiting for the kingdom, who
knew that sixty-nine weeks of Daniel's prophecy of the
times and the seasons had expired, and who were concerned as to the fulfillment of the brief period that was
left and the ushering in of the kingdom. In verses 4 to
8 we have what in a general way covers this entire dispensation:

"And Jesus answered and said unto them, Take
heed that no man deceive you. For many shall come
in my name, saying, I am Christ; and shall deceive
many. And ye shall hear of wars and rumors of
wars: see that ye be not troubled; for all these things
must come to pass, but the end is not yet. For nation
shall rise against nation, and kingdom against kingdom: and there shall be famines, and pestilences, and
earthquakes, in divers places. All these are the beginning of sorrows" (Matthew 24:4-8).

But these will be the actual conditions prevailing in the first part of Daniel's seventieth week, for the Great Tribulation in its intensity occupies only the last three and one-half years, or 1,260 days. The first half, or forty-two months, will be taken up with providential judgments leading up to that awful hour of trial. At first the distress on earth will be occasioned by the disrupted condition of things when, following the Rapture of the Church, God once more takes up Israel, and the Gentile nations will be in turmoil and conflict. This will be followed by a time of great testing for the remnant of Israel, who will be called out in that day to be God's witnesses in the earth. It is particularly to these that verses 9 to 14 apply:

> "Then shall they deliver you up to be afflicted, and shall kill you: and ye shall be hated of all nations for my name's sake. And then shall many be offended, and shall betray one another, and shall hate one another. And many false prophets shall rise, and shall deceive many. And because iniquity shall abound, the love of many shall wax cold. But he that shall endure unto the end, the same shall be saved. And this gospel of the kingdom shall be preached in all the world for a witness unto all nations; and then shall the end come" (Matthew 24:9-14).

Notice that He speaks here of the good news which these Jewish messengers are to carry throughout the world, called distinctively "the gospel of the kingdom." There is, of course, only one Gospel, but that Gospel presents different aspects at different times. The Gospel is God's message concerning His blessed Son. It was proclaimed in the Garden of Eden when God declared: "The seed of the woman shall bruise the serpent's head."

It was preached to Abraham when He said: "In thy seed shall all the nations of the earth be blessed." The Old Testament prophets were Gospel preachers as they told of the coming Messiah. When John the Baptist appeared, his voice rang out, proclaiming: "Repent ye: for the kingdom of heaven is at hand." On the other hand, let us never forget that it was also John the Baptist who preached the Gospel of grace when he said, "I saw and bear record that this is the Son of God. Behold the Lamb of God, which taketh away the sin of the world." The Lord Jesus went about proclaiming the Gospel of the kingdom. He presented Himself to Israel as God's King, but they refused Him. Then He turned to the weary multitudes and said, "Come unto me, all ye that labour and are heavy laden, and I will give you rest." And we must not forget that though John's Gospel was written several decades later than the Synoptics, yet it records the preaching and teaching of our blessed Lord in regard to the Gospel of grace while He was going about through the land of Palestine proclaiming the kingdom.

Here in Matthew 24 we have no apparent break in the testimony. If we can understand that the Great Parenthesis comes in between our Lord's rejection and the beginning of the fulfillment of this Olivet Discourse, everything will be clear. In that day of trial, God will raise up a special testimony in Israel even as we are told in the book of Daniel. "They that be wise shall shine as the brightness of the firmament; and they that turn many to righteousness as the stars for ever and ever . . . Many shall be purified, and made white, and tried;

but the wicked shall do wickedly: and none of the
wicked shall understand; but the wise shall understand"
(Daniel 12:3, 10). These wise ones in Israel will proclaim the Gospel of the kingdom. Their witness will go
on until all nations have heard the testimony. Then the
final end of the age will come.

In writing as I have done, I trust no one will misuse
the truth which I am here seeking to present by endeavor-
ing to excuse themselves from present missionary activity
on the ground that it will be Israel's business to proclaim
the Gospel of the kingdom in a coming day. Our Lord
seems to have purposely led Mark to record His saying
a little differently. In Mark 13:10 we read: "And the
gospel must first be published among all nations." This
is a very broad statement, and we know from what the
Spirit of God afterwards revealed that it is our responsibility to carry the Gospel everywhere during this intervening period before Israel's remnant testimony will
be given to the people of the end-times.

Verse 15 of our chapter brings us to the midst of
the week and introduces the last three and one-half
dreadful years. Notice our Lord's words:

> "When ye therefore shall see the abomination of
> desolation, spoken of by Daniel the prophet, stand in
> the holy place, (whoso readeth, let him understand:)
> then let them which be in Judaea flee into the moun-
> tains: let him which is on the housetop not come
> down to take anything out of his house: neither let
> him which is in the field return back to take his
> clothes. And woe unto them that are with child, and
> to them that give suck in those days! But pray ye
> that your flight be not in the winter, neither on the
> sabbath day: for then shall be great tribulation, such

as was not since the beginning of the world to this time, no, nor ever shall be. And except those days should be shortened, there should no flesh be saved: but for the elect's sake those days shall be shortened. Then if any man shall say unto you, Lo, here is Christ, or there; believe it not. For there shall arise false Christs, and false prophets, and shall shew great signs and wonders; insomuch that, if it were possible, they shall deceive the very elect. Behold, I have told you before. Wherefore if they shall say unto you, Behold, he is in the desert; go not forth: behold, he is in the secret chambers; believe it not" (Matthew 24:15-26).

The abomination of desolation spoken of here is not to be confounded with the transgression of desolation of Daniel 8:13. That had to do with the polluting of the Sanctuary by the setting up of an idol in the Holy Place in the days of Antiochus Epiphanes, but this reference is to Daniel 12:11-12:

> "And from the time that the daily sacrifice shall be taken away, and the abomination that maketh desolate set up, there shall be a thousand two hundred and ninety days. Blessed is he that waiteth, and cometh to the thousand three hundred and five and thirty days" (Daniel 12:11-12).

That is, the setting up of the abomination of desolation, whatever its full meaning may be, will be the signal for the remnant of the latter days, to let them know that in 1,260 days the Great Tribulation will be over, and in thirty days more the new order of things will have come in. The additional time, bringing the waiting period up to 1,335 days, may have to do with the reinstitution of Jehovah's worship in Jerusalem. These verses we have quoted above have nothing to do with the destruction of Jerusalem in the past, as one may see by comparing them with Luke 21, but they describe a future siege of Jerusalem, when the Roman prince and the Antichrist have been manifested. Then shall be great tribulation such as was not since the beginning of the world, no, nor ever shall be. Then Satan will raise up false Christs and false prophets to seek to deceive the waiting remnant, but the Lord has forewarned them not to believe the lying testimonies of Satan-inspired leaders in that day.

His Coming will be in manifested glory at the close of the tribulation period, as we read in verses 27 to 31.

"For as the lightning cometh out of the east, and shineth even unto the west; so shall also the coming of the Son of man be. For wheresoever the carcass is, there will the eagles be gathered together. Immediately after the tribulation of those days shall the sun be darkened, and the moon shall not give her light, and the stars shall fall from heaven, and the powers of the heavens shall be shaken: and then shall appear the sign of the Son of man in heaven: and then shall all the tribes of the earth mourn, and they shall see the Son of man coming in the clouds of heaven with power and great glory. And he shall send his angels with a great sound of a trumpet, and they shall gather together his elect from the four winds, from one end of heaven to the other" (Matthew 24:27-31).

I am not attempting a careful exegesis of this chapter, but am merely drawing attention to its broad outlines. A few things, however, should be noticed before leaving it. The twenty-eighth verse evidently refers to the city of Jerusalem which will be the carcass in that day, and against it the eagles, or "vultures," the carrion-devouring armies of the nations, will be gathered. There will be portentious signs in the heavens when the Son of Man appears in glory. The tribes of the land will mourn, as Zechariah has foretold in his twelfth chapter, And men will "see the Son of man coming in the clouds of heaven with power and great glory." This is something altogether different from the Rapture of the Church as portrayed in I Corinthians 15 and in I Thessalonians 4. There is no gathering of saints to Him in the heavens here, but He sends forth His angels with the great sound of a trumpet, and they gather His elect together from the four winds, from one end of heaven to the other. These are not the heavenly saints but the earthly elect, the 144,000 of Israel and the great number of redeemed Gentiles as set forth in Revelation 7. They will be gathered to Christ Himself when He appears in Jerusalem and His feet stand upon the Mount of Olives, before His foes are dealt with in judgment.

It will not be necessary for our present purpose to pursue the further study of this chapter, interesting as it is. The inquiring reader can find many excellent helps if he desires to go into the matter carefully.* My object has been simply to show that the key to our Lord's prophecy is the ninth chapter of the book of Daniel. The Great Parenthesis there indicated, if taken into account when reading this remarkable chapter, makes everything perfectly plain.

---

* I am glad to recommend three excellent books on the Gospel of Matthew: *Lectures on Matthew*, by William Kelly, and the expositions by Dr. A. C. Gaebelein and Dr. E. Schuyler English. Any of these will prove helpful to the student of prophecy who desires a careful explanation of this portion of the Word.

CHAPTER VI

THE FIRST CHURCH COUNCIL;
THE PARENTHESIS RECOGNIZED
BY THE APOSTLES

Acts 15 is the great dispensational chapter of that book. It occupies a unique place in the New Testament, and is a very distinct help in the understanding of God's present work of grace and His future plans for Israel and the world.

When Paul returned to Antioch at the conclusion of his first missionary journey, we are told that the whole Church was gathered together, to whom he and Barnabas "rehearsed all that God had done with them, and how he had opened the door of faith unto the Gentiles" (Acts 14:27). For some time afterwards they continued in that same city, teaching and enjoying the fellowship of the saints, but soon a discordant note was introduced, destroying the spiritual harmony which up to that time had prevailed.

We are told in the first verse of chapter 15: "And certain men which came down from Judaea taught the brethren, and said, Except ye be circumcised after the manner of Moses, ye cannot be saved." It is evident that these men maintained they acted under apostolic authority and were the official representatives of the Church at Jerusalem. They were evidently rigid Jews of the Pharisaic type who had professed conversion to Christ and had been identified with the churches in

Judaea. Having only the Old Testament, they based all their conclusions upon it. We need to remember, in order not to judge them too harshly, that so far as we have definite information, not one book of the New Testament had yet been written. There is a bare possibility that Matthew or Mark or perhaps both might be exceptions to this, but of that we have no proof. When these brethren or others referred to the Scriptures, it was necessarily the Old Testament which they had in mind. From the Old Testament they learned that God had made a covenant of grace with Abraham, had promised that all nations would be blessed through his Seed, and had given the ordinance of circumcision as the outward sign that was to separate the covenant people from the rest of the world.

Of course, from the beginning the apostles had taught, as Peter did, the setting aside of the nation of Israel because of their rejection of Messiah, and called upon those who trusted Him to separate themselves by baptism from the apostate part of the nation, and thus save themselves from that untoward generation and the judgment soon to fall upon it; but we can well understand that many Jewish believers might not have grasped the full implication of this, nor have recognized the fact that God was doing an altogether new thing not predicted in Old Testament times.

There is, therefore, no reason to question the sincerity of these Judaean emissaries who doubtless thought that Paul and Barnabas were playing fast and loose with the divine order in not insisting that the Gentile believers accept the sign of the Abrahamic covenant and thus identify themselves with the remnant of the chosen people.

There was evidently considerable discussion in the Antiochian Church regarding the whole matter, as a result of which Paul and Barnabas were asked to go with some others directly to Jerusalem and confer there with the apostles and elders about this question. As they made their way toward their appointed destination, they passed through Phenice and Samaria, declaring whenever they came in contact with Christian assemblies how God had wrought in power in converting the heathen from among the Gentiles. The news of this brought great joy, we are told, unto all the brethren. It is evident that the questions raised by the men from Judæa had not come before these churches as they made no mention of bringing such demands to bear upon the young converts, but simply rejoiced in what God had done for them.

In verse 4 we are told that "when they were come to Jerusalem, they were received of the church, and of the apostles and elders, and they declared all things that God had done with them." This was evidently in a large open meeting where a great number of the Jerusalem Christians gathered together to receive them and to welcome them in their midst. In this meeting no doctrinal matters or questions of ceremonial observances were discussed until after Paul and Barnabas had given their testimony to the way in which God had wrought through their ministry to the Gentiles. After this we are told: "There rose up certain of the sect of the Pharisees which believed, saying, That it was needful to circumcise them,

and to command them to keep the law of Moses."
These men, like the others who had appeared at Antioch,
felt sure of their ground for they could appeal directly
to Old Testament Scripture, and they took it for granted
that God was now doing what He had promised to do
through the prophets, that is, to give the knowledge of
His salvation to the Gentiles, but that they would receive
blessing through Israel and would be united to them as
children of the covenant by taking upon them the outward sign to which they referred. See Isaiah 56:6;
60:3-5; Zech. 8:23, to which many other passages might
be added.

Apparently the leaders decided not to debate the
question at that time nor to attempt to handle it in a large
open meeting, for in verse 6 we read: "The apostles and
elders came together for to consider of this matter."
This would be much wiser, of course, than putting the
question up to the entire body of believers, many of
whom would have a very imperfect understanding of the
Gospel itself and a very slight knowledge of the Holy
Scriptures. The apostles appointed by the Lord Jesus
to carry the message into all the world and those who
had been selected as elders to guide the affairs of the
local churches met in council with Paul and Barnabas
and their associates to go into the matter dispassionately
and carefully.

We can see, as we read on, that even these brethren
were not of one mind, for we are told that there was
"much disputing." How long this went on we do not
know, but eventually the Apostle Peter took the floor

and reminded them how God had in a very clear and
definite way sent him to the Gentiles in the house of
Cornelius, but that there had then been no commandment
to circumcise the believers or to put them under the
yoke of the law of Moses. I quote Peter's address in
full so far as we have it here. Doubtless verses 7 to 11
give us but an abbreviation of what he presented to the
assembled company:

> "Men and brethren, ye know how that a good
> while ago God made choice among us, that the
> Gentiles by my mouth should hear the word of the
> gospel, and believe. And God, which knoweth the
> hearts, bare them witness, giving them the Holy
> Ghost, even as he did unto us; and put no difference
> between us and them, purifying their hearts by faith.
> Now therefore why tempt ye God, to put a yoke
> upon the neck of the disciples, which neither our
> fathers nor we were able to bear? But we believe
> that through the grace of the Lord Jesus Christ we
> shall be saved, even as they" (Acts 15:7-11).

Observe how carefully the Apostle Peter presented
his case. It was God who had chosen him to go to the
Gentiles, that through his lips they should hear the word
of the Gospel and put their trust in the Lord Jesus Christ.
As he was preaching, Cornelius and his household believed the message, and immediately God, who reads the
hearts, recognized their faith and gave them the Holy
Spirit in the same way in which He gave it to the one
hundred and twenty of Israel on the day of Pentecost.
The fact that these were uncircumcised Gentiles and
that those were circumcised Jews made no difference
whatever to God. It was the state of the heart upon
which He looked, and so Peter insists that He did not

distinguish between the two groups, but purified their hearts by faith, that is, regenerated them when they believed the Gospel. If this satisfied God, why should it not satisfy the Jewish Christians? Were they not tempting God when they sought now to put the yoke of the law upon the neck of these young believers from among the Gentiles, a yoke which they themselves, as Jews, had always found burdensome?

Then Peter closes in a remarkable way. He says: "We believe that through the grace of the Lord Jesus Christ we shall be saved, even as they." We might well expect that he would have turned it completely around. He might have said: "We believe that they shall be saved even as we"; but he does not do that. He declares that the Jews, despite all their privileges, are to be saved on the same basis of pure grace as idolatrous or philosophical Gentiles who put their trust in the Lord Jesus Christ.

This was evidently so convincing that the legalists were nonplused and for the moment knew not how to reply. Taking advantage of the silence, Barnabas and Paul, one after the other, addressed the audience. Note that Barnabas came first in this case as he was well known to the Jerusalem Christians and was highly esteemed for his godliness and righteous life. Paul, who was doubtless more or less under suspicion on the part of some, followed. Both gave the same marvelous testimony to the mighty wonder-working power of God as He wrought among the Gentiles. In this they corroborated the testimony given by Peter.

We can imagine the rigid Pharisaic Christian Jews
silenced but unconvinced. In their own minds they
would be saying, "But we have the Word of God on
our side. Regardless of the remarkable experiences
Peter and Barnabas and Paul can relate, it is very definitely stated in Scripture that those whom God recognizes as His covenant people are to be marked out from
the rest of the world by the covenant sign. Moreover,
who has been authorized to set aside the commands of the
Law, a Law given by God Himself when He appeared to
Moses on Sinai?" They knew, of course, that there
were many promises in the Old Testament of blessing
for the Gentiles. They knew that the day was yet to
come when all the nations of the world would recognize
in the Lord Jesus Christ God's King, but when that day
came, Israel was to have the pre-eminent place. There
was no proof that God's attitude would be changed in
regard to the matters in question. The presumption was
that all the Gentiles would in a certain sense become as
Jews when together they should all enjoy the blessings
of Messiah's reign. Yet these brethren must have been
puzzled to explain the way in which God was now working among the Gentiles and His apparent indifference
regarding what to them seemed so important.

James, however, had the key to the entire situation.
We have a brief outline of his speech given in verses
13 to 21:

> "Men and brethren, hearken unto me: Simeon hath
> declared how God at the first did visit the Gentiles,
> to take out of them a people for his name. And to
> this agree the words of the prophets; as it is written,

After this I will return, and will build again the tabernacle of David, which is fallen down; and I will build again the ruins thereof, and I will set it up: that the residue of men might seek after the Lord, and all the Gentiles, upon whom my name is called, saith the Lord, who doeth all these things. Known unto God are all his works from the beginning of the world. Wherefore my sentence is, that we trouble not them, which from among the Gentiles are turned to God: but that we write unto them, that they abstain from pollutions of idols, and from fornication, and from things strangled, and from blood. For Moses of old time hath in every city them that preach him, being read in the synagogues every sabbath day" (Acts 15:13-21).

He refers to what Peter had already told them, but he uses an expression which is of great interest to us, and was indeed the explanation to the present work of grace. "God," he says, "at the first did visit the Gentiles, to take out of them a people for his name." Now this is not the conversion of the Gentiles as predicted in the Old Testament. The taking out of a people, instead of the conversion of the nations as such, was something very different from that revealed by the prophets. This spoke of a special election from among the Gentiles and that doubtless for a particular purpose. This is the work that God is doing now. While the messengers of the Gospel are to carry it to all nations, God's present object is not the conversion of the nations through this testimony but that all men may have an opportunity to come to Christ if they will, but He who knows the end from the beginning has foreseen the fact that only a small number comparatively would actually receive the message in faith, and trust the Lord Jesus Christ as their

Saviour. This company is designated throughout the book of Acts as the Church of God, and of the Church of God as such we hear nothing in the Old Testament prophecies.

But now observe how James harmonizes the present work of God in taking an elect people out from among the nations and the prophecies of the conversion of all the nations in some future day. He refers his hearers to the prophecy of Amos as recorded in chapter 9, verses 11 and 12: "After this I will return." This is not exactly the way Amos wrote it, but James is quoting from the Septuagint, and he recognizes the correctness of the expression. "After this," that is, after the present work of God in taking a people out from among the nations is concluded, Messiah will return again. Then when He comes back He will build once more the Tabernacle of David which has been for so long set aside. He will raise up the throne of David again and fulfill the prophecies made to that man after His own heart. It will be in that day that the residue will seek after the Lord and all the Gentiles upon whom His Name will then be called.

This made everything clear. James, you see, recognized and explained the Great Parenthesis in God's dealings with Israel. He showed that the Church of God had been called out and was bearing its witness in that parenthetic period. When it shall come to a close, the Lord will return again and fulfill all the prophecies connected with Israel's restoration and the salvation of the nations of the world. And so he exclaims, "Known unto God are all his works from the beginning of the world."

God is working according to a plan, and that plan was partly unfolded in Old Testament times, but now has been fully made known. In the light of the revelation thus given, James suggested that no further pressure should be brought upon the Gentiles to make them conform to Jewish rites or ceremonies, but that they should be called upon simply to abstain from the evils connected with idolatry, from the immorality that was so common among the nations, and from unclean foods which to their Jewish brethren were abhorrent. If any of the Gentile believers wished to know more of the teachings of the Law, they could easily find enlightenment, for in virtually every city there were synagogues in which the Law of Moses was read and taught, and any who desired could go in to hear.

This settled the matter at least for the present, and a letter was drawn up and sent out to the Gentiles to put their minds at rest regarding the teaching of the legalists who were seeking to turn them away from their liberty in Christ. We have the letter given in verses 23 to 29:

> "And they wrote letters by them after this manner; The apostles and elders and brethren send greeting unto the brethren which are of the Gentiles in Antioch and Syria and Cilicia: Forasmuch as we have heard, that certain which went out from us have troubled you with words, subverting your souls, saying, Ye must be circumcised, and keep the law: to whom we gave no such commandment: it seemed good unto us, being assembled with one accord, to send chosen men unto you with our beloved Barnabas and Paul, men that have hazarded their lives for the name of our Lord Jesus Christ. We have sent therefore Judas and Silas, who shall also tell you the same things

by mouth. For it seemed good to the Holy Ghost,
and to us, to lay upon you no greater burden than
these necessary things; that ye abstain from meats
offered to idols, and from blood, and from things
strangled, and from fornication: from which if ye
keep yourselves, ye shall do well. Fare ye well"
(Acts 15:23-29).

It must have been with great joy and light hearts that
Barnabas and Paul and their companions left Jerusalem
and returned to Antioch. The truth for which they had
been contending for so long was now acknowledged by
the brethren at Jerusalem, and they could go on preaching with the full assurance that their testimony was en-
dorsed by those who had been in Christ before them.
They immediately gathered the C h u r c h together, to
whom the letter was read, and all rejoiced for the con-
solation that it brought. It is true that later on further
trouble developed, because legalism is a form of leaven,
and it is in the nature of leaven to work; and so we have
the Epistle to the Galatians, written to Gentile believers
some years later in order to counteract the contentious
propaganda of certain Jews who still insisted on pressing
upon the Gentiles the necessity of conforming to the Law
of Moses. That letter is in itself the very best answer
to legality of every description.

The pitiable thing is that in the centuries that have
elapsed since, the Judaizing of the Church has gone on in
an amazing way until in many places the Gospel of the
grace of God is looked upon as though it were a strange
new heresy, whereas the effort of men to procure justification by human merit and sanctification by attention to
religious rites and ceremonies is accepted as the ortho-

dox position. It only shows how hard it is for these poor hearts of ours to abide in the truth of the grace of God. We so readily seek some other ground of approach to God and fitness for His presence than that of pure, unadulterated grace as set forth in the work of our Lord Jesus Christ and the purifying power of the Holy Spirit. One great reason for this is that so many fail to differentiate between the covenant of works given at Sinai and the grace of God as revealed in the Lord Jesus Christ. We read in John 1, verse 17: "The law was given by Moses, but grace and truth came by Jesus Christ." That Law, Paul tells us in the Galatian letter, was a child-leader designed to guide the steps of the people of God in the days of their nonage until Christ Himself should come. Now that He has come there is no further need of the child-leader, but all that is required both for justification and sanctification is found in the risen Christ, who, of God "is made unto us wisdom, and righteousness, sanctification and redemption" (I Cor. 1:30).

Chapter VII

THE PARENTHETICAL PERIOD IN ISRAEL'S ECCLESIASTICAL YEAR

Before going on to examine the parenthetical part of the Epistle to the Romans which deals with God's past, present and future ways with Israel, there is another Old Testament Scripture to which we should turn our attention for further corroboration of the undisclosed present period which we have been considering.

In the twenty-third chapter of the book of Leviticus we have the feasts or "set times" of Jehovah. This chapter has well been called Israel's ecclesiastical year, using the term "ecclesiastical" in the sense in which it is often used today as designating the special festivals of the professing Church. So far as Christians are concerned, the Word of God does not indicate any such festivals for their observance, and the more we make of them the more we are likely to come under the censure of the Apostle to the Gentiles as set forth in the Epistle to the Galatians: "Ye observe days, and months, and times, and years. I am afraid of you, lest I have bestowed upon you labour in vain" (Galatians 4:10-11).

But with Israel it was otherwise. In the legal dispensation God Himself appointed certain weekly and annual festivals which were to be faithfully observed during all that dispensation, and each of which had a typical significance. In the third verse of this twenty-third chapter of Leviticus we have the "sabbath of rest," which is called a "holy convocation," in which no work was to be done. This, of course, was the weekly "set time" and was observed with a double purpose. First, it was a recognition of Jehovah's creation rest as indicated in Exodus 20, verses 8 to 11:

> "Remember the sabbath day, to keep it holy. Six days shalt thou labour, and do all thy work: but the seventh day is the sabbath of the Lord thy God: in it thou shalt not do any work, thou, nor thy son, nor thy daughter, thy manservant, nor thy maidservant, nor thy cattle, nor thy stranger that is within thy gates: for in six days the Lord made heaven and earth, the sea, and all that in them is, and rested the seventh day: wherefore the Lord blessed the sabbath day, and hallowed it" (Exodus 20:8-11).

Then in Deuteronomy 5, where we have the reiteration of the Ten Commandments, another reason is given for the observance of the Sabbath. We read in verse 15: "And remember that thou wast a servant in the land of Egypt, and that the Lord thy God brought thee out thence through a mighty hand and by a stretched out arm: therefore the Lord thy God commanded thee to keep the sabbath day." This second reason makes one thing very definite, namely, that the Ten Commandments as such were never given to the Gentiles but solely to Israel, the covenant people. Of course, when the Gentiles became familiar with them, it was their responsibility to maintain the high moral standards there set forth, but nowhere are we told that the Sabbath was a sign of God's covenant with the nations.

It had both a backward and a forward aspect. Looking forward, it typified the rest that remains for the people of God, a Sabbath Rest which will be enjoyed eternally by all who know Christ as Saviour, as indicated in Hebrews 4, verses 4 to 9.

The reason that the Sabbath occupies the first place in this list of the feasts of Jehovah is because God's first thought for mankind is His last. He has ever had before Him the time when in the new heavens and the new earth He will dwell with His people in a condition of perfection, after all the varied experiences through which men shall pass during their sojourn in this world.

In verse 4 we read: "These are the feasts of the Lord, even holy convocations, which ye shall proclaim in their seasons." The word *feasts* here is somewhat misleading. We think of a feast as a time of merriment and enjoyment, possibly even as an occasion when we regale ourselves with toothsome viands; but no such thought is necessarily connected with the word used here. It would be better to translate it "set times" or "appointed seasons," because some of these so-called feasts were actually fasts, when the people were to refrain from food and drink as they meditated upon their sins and transgressions. They were, however, definite, appointed seasons to be observed from year to year.

As we read through the chapter, we notice that three of these "set times" were to be observed in the spring of the year, and all of these were types of great events which have already had a glorious fulfillment. First we are told:

> "In the fourteenth day of the first month at even
> is the Lord's passover. And on the fifteenth day of
> the same month is the feast of unleavened bread unto
> the Lord: seven days ye must eat unleavened bread.
> In the first day ye shall have an holy convocation: ye
> shall do no servile work therein. But ye shall offer
> an offering made by fire unto the Lord seven days:
> in the seventh day is an holy convocation: ye shall
> do no servile work therein" (Lev. 23:5-8).

The Passover and the Feast of Unleavened Bread were
intimately connected. We do not have to guess at the
meaning of either for when we turn to I Corinthians 5,
verses 6 to 8, we read:

> "Your glorying is not good. Know ye not that a
> little leaven leaveneth the whole lump? Purge out
> therefore the old leaven, that ye may be a new lump,
> as ye are unleavened. For even Christ our passover
> is sacrificed for us: therefore let us keep the feast,
> not with old leaven, neither with the leaven of malice
> and wickedness; but with the unleavened bread of
> sincerity and truth" (I Cor. 5:6-8).

The Passover, then, typified the death of our Lord
Jesus Christ, God's unblemished, spotless Lamb who
gave Himself for us in order that divine judgment might
never fall upon us. To Israel in Egypt, in connection
with the first Passover and the sprinkling of blood, Jehovah said: "When I see the blood, I will pass over
you." This points to the cross of Christ, and is the great
truth that gives rest to every believing heart.

The fourteenth day of the first month was in the early
spring, for Israel's sacred year began at that time. The
month Abib, or "Green Ears," answers, generally speaking, to the last part of our March and the first half of
April. It was then that the Passover was to be observed,

and when we come to the New Testament we find that our Lord Jesus Christ observed this feast Himself with His disciples on the first evening of the fourteenth of Abib, and in the morning of the same day He was nailed upon the cross, and in the afternoon He died as the great Paschal Lamb. The Jewish day was from sunset to sunset, and the Passover was to be slain between the two evenings, as we are told in Exodus 12; so our Lord ate the Passover and died as the Paschal Lamb between the two evenings. Thus the type was completely fulfilled.

Now we who have put our trust in Him are called to purge away all leaven, and leaven is ever in Scripture a type of evil. Our Lord warned His disciples to beware of the leaven of the Pharisees, which is hypocrisy and self-righteousness; of the leaven of the Sadducees, which is false doctrine; and of the leaven of Herod, which is worldliness and political corruption. And in the passage already referred to in First Corinthians, we read of the leaven of malice and wickedness. In Galatians and in First Corinthians, Paul uses the expression, "A little leaven leaveneth the whole lump." In the one case he refers to false doctrine which, if not checked, permeates the mass, and in the other to immorality which, if not judged in the light of the cross of Christ, will have a most devastating effect upon those who are inclined to be led astray. It is for us, therefore, as the redeemed of the Lord, redeemed not with corruptible things such as silver and gold but with the precious blood of Christ, to be careful to put all leaven out of our lives and so to walk before God in holiness and truth. This is to keep

the Feast of Unleavened Bread according to the divine
appointment for our dispensation.

We come next to the Feast of Firstfruits.   In verses
9 to 14 we read:

> "And the Lord spake unto Moses, saying, Speak
> unto the children of Israel, and say unto them, When
> ye be come into the land which I give unto you, and
> shall reap the harvest thereof, then ye shall bring
> a sheaf of the firstfruits of your harvest unto the
> priest: and he shall wave the sheaf before the Lord,
> to be accepted for you: on the morrow after the sab-
> bath the priest shall wave it. And ye shall offer that
> day when ye wave the sheaf and the lamb without
> blemish of the first year for a burnt-offering unto
> the Lord. And the meat-offering thereof shall be
> two tenth deals of fine flour mingled with oil, an
> offering made by fire unto the Lord for a sweet
> savour: and the drink-offering thereof shall be of
> wine, the fourth part of an hin. And ye shall eat
> neither bread, nor parched corn, nor green ears, until
> the selfsame day that ye have brought an offering
> unto your God: it shall be a statute for ever through-
> out your generations in all your dwellings" (Leviti-
> cus 23:9-14).

Again we are not left to our own imagination when
we ask: "What is the meaning of this feast?" For when
we turn to First Corinthians 15, that great resurrection
chapter in which the Apostle is emphasizing the importance of the truth of Christ's having been raised from the
dead, we see that in verse 20 he says: "But now is Christ
risen from the dead, and become the firstfruits of them
that slept." Then again in verses 22 and 23:

> "For as in Adam all die, even so in Christ shall all
> be made alive. But every man in his own order:
> Christ the firstfruits; afterward they that are Christ's
> at his coming" (I Corinthians 15:22-23).

The presentation of the firstfruits, then, typified the rising of Christ from the dead and His acceptance by God the Father after He had completed the work upon which our redemption rests.

And notice in verse 11 of our chapter, it was on the morrow after the Sabbath that the priest was to present the firstfruits before God. Now remember that our Lord Jesus Christ died on Passover Day and was raised again at the beginning of the first day of the week following. We can see how God here pictures the setting aside of the Sabbath of the Law and the bringing in of what the Apostle John calls, in Revelation 1, "the Lord's day." From Psalm 118, we infer that the Spirit of God puts special honor upon this day because of the glorious event which was then to take place. In verse 22 we have the rejection of Christ involving His crucifixion: "The stone which the builders refused is become the head stone of the corner." His resurrection and the sanctity of the new day are implied in verses 23 and 24: "This is the Lord's doing; it is marvelous in our eyes. This is the day which the Lord hath made; we will rejoice and be glad in it."

Throughout the last Sabbath of the Jews which God ever recognized, no one on earth could possibly know whether redemption was a success or not. The body of the Lord Jesus Christ after His death upon the cross lay in Joseph's new tomb. Had He not come forth in resurrection on the first day of the week, all His declarations in regard to the great work He came to do would have been proved false. It was His resurrection which made it manifest that He was indeed the promised Saviour of

mankind.   He was delivered up to death for our of-
fences and was raised again for our justification.   Christ
having completed the work that saves, God bore witness
to His delight in His Son and His satisfaction in the work
he had accomplished by raising Him from the dead.
The Lord Jesus as the risen One has been accepted of
the Father, and all who believe are accepted in Him.

There is much more in this section that we could dwell
upon, but I pass over it now because my chief object is
to show how what we have here links up with what we
have already been considering.

In the next section we have the Feast of Pentecost.
Note verses 15 to 22:

> "And ye shall count unto you from the morrow
> after the sabbath, from the day that ye brought the
> sheaf of the wave-offering; seven sabbaths shall be
> complete: even unto the morrow after the seventh
> sabbath shall ye number fifty days; and ye shall offer
> a new meat-offering unto the Lord. Ye shall bring
> out of your habitations two wave-loaves of two tenth
> deals: they shall be of fine flour; they shall be baken
> with leaven, they are the firstfruits unto the Lord.
> And ye shall offer with the bread seven lambs with-
> out blemish of the first year, and one young bullock,
> and two rams: they shall be for a burnt-offering
> unto the Lord, with their meat-offering, and their
> drink-offerings, even an offering made by fire, of
> sweet savour unto the Lord. Then ye shall sacrifice
> one kid of the goats for a sin-offering, and two lambs
> of the first year for a sacrifice of peace-offerings.
> And the priest shall wave them with the bread of
> the firstfruits for a wave-offering before the Lord,
> with the two lambs: they shall be holy to the Lord
> for the priest. And ye shall proclaim on the self-
> same day, that it may be an holy convocation unto

you: ye shall do no servile work therein: it shall be
a statute for ever in all your dwellings throughout
your generations. And when ye reap the harvest of
your land, thou shalt not make clean riddance of the
corners of thy field when thou reapest, neither shalt
thou gather any gleaning of thy harvest: thou shalt
leave them unto the poor, and to the stranger: I am
the Lord your God" (Leviticus 23:15-22).

This feast took place fifty days after that of the firstfruits. The word "pentecost," of course, indicates this,
and we are told definitely that the Israelites were to
count from the morrow after the Sabbath when they
brought the sheaf of the wave offering until seven Sabbaths had passed. Then upon the morrow after the
seventh Sabbath they were to bring a new *meal* offering
unto the Lord. This is the better translation here. We
generally think of meat as flesh, but when the Authorized
Version was translated, the word still had its original
meaning of food, so that this was the food offering and
was composed of meal. Two wave loaves were to be
presented before the Lord. Unlike the ordinary meal
offering, which typified our Lord Jesus Christ and in
which there was to be no leaven, these wave loaves were
to be baked with leaven, and they are called also "firstfruits unto the Lord." It is clear, then, that they typify
not Christ Himself but believers in Christ in whom there
is a sinful nature (as there was not in Him), but that
nature has been judged in the light of the cross of Christ
and therefore the leaven is conceived of as baked. They
represent, then, redeemed sinners who have been born
of God, even as we read in James 1, verse 18: "Of his
own will begat he us with the word of truth, that we
should be a kind of firstfruits of his creatures."

Now, we have the fulfillment of this feast on the day
of Pentecost as recorded in the second chapter of the
book of Acts. It was then that our Lord baptized believers by the Holy Spirit, and this baptism, we are
told in First Corinthians 12, verse 13, formed the one
body which is the Church of this dispensation. It is well
to notice the full statement in First Corinthians:

> "For as the body is one, and hath many members,
> and all the members of that one body, being many,
> are one body: so also is Christ. For by one Spirit
> are we all baptized into one body, whether we be
> Jews or Gentiles, whether we be bond or free; and
> have been all made to drink into one Spirit" (I Cor-
> inthians 12:12-13).

The two loaves undoubtedly picture the two groups
— Jew and Gentile. Both alike were sinners; both had
to judge their sins in the light of the cross; both are
accepted by God in all the value of the work of His Son.
There is no intimation here, however, that both would
form one body, nor was that made known on the day
of Pentecost, but through the Apostle Paul, as the chosen
vessel of testimony to the Gentiles, this truth was later
made known as the dispensation progressed.

And now we come to something of intense interest
for those who have followed me in this series of studies
thus far. These three feasts, which all have to do with
the blessing of the people of God in this age, all took
place in the spring of the year. There were no more
such "set times" until the seventh month, which would
answer to our September-October, and then there were
three more feasts following one another in quick succes-
sion and intimately linked together. But all of them

have to do particularly with God's future dealings with the nation of Israel, so that we have a period of some five months in which there were no special "set times" indicated. This long period fits in perfectly with the parenthesis in God's prophetic plan which we have seen must be taken into account in so many places if we are to rightly apprehend what God is doing now.

When the summer was over and the close of the year had come, God commanded His people to observe the Feast of Trumpets. Notice verses 23 to 25. This ordinance of the blowing of trumpets on the first day of the seventh month is observed by the Jews today for the ushering in of the new civil year as distinguished from the ecclesiastical year. It is called the Feast of Rosh-Hashana. On this day the trumpets are blown, indicating the ushering in of a new period of time. This has to do entirely with Israel. It signifies the blowing of the great trumpet when God's earthly people who have wandered from Him for so long will be called back to Himself and to their land to enter upon Millennial blessedness. Many Scriptures refer to this, a few of which we will mention here:

> "All ye inhabitants of the world, and dwellers on the earth, see ye, when he lifteth up an ensign on the mountains; and when he bloweth a trumpet, hear ye. For so the Lord said unto me, I will take my rest, and I will consider in my dwelling place like a clear heat upon herbs, and like a cloud of dew in the heat of harvest. For afore the harvest, when the bud is perfect, and the sour grape is ripening in the flower, he shall both cut off the sprigs with pruning hooks, and take away and cut down the branches. They shall

be left together unto the fowls of the mountains, and
to the beasts of the earth: and the fowls shall summer upon them, and all the beasts of the earth shall
winter upon them. In that time shall the present be
brought unto the Lord of hosts of a people scattered
and peeled, and from a people terrible from their
beginning hitherto; a nation meted out and trodden
under foot, whose land the rivers have spoiled, to
the place of the name of the Lord of hosts, the mount
Zion" (Isaiah 18:3-7).

This passage clearly refers to the call which will go
out from the Lord after the Church Age is past, sum-
moning His scattered people Israel to return to Himself
and to their inheritance. Again in Isaiah 27:12-13 we
read:

"And it shall come to pass in that day, that the
Lord shall beat off from the channel of the river unto
the stream of Egypt, and ye shall be gathered one by
one, O ye children of Israel. And it shall come to
pass in that day, that the great trumpet shall be
blown, and they shall come which were ready to perish in the land of Assyria, and the outcasts in the
land of Egypt, and shall worship the Lord in the
holy mount at Jerusalem."

Surely these words need no explanation. They are absolutely clear and tell us in no uncertain way that the
blowing of the trumpet has to do with Israel's return.

In the second chapter of Joel, verses 1 and 2, we see
that when this trumpet is blown, the people of Israel
will be in the midst of great tribulation and distress such
as they have never previously known. The attempt has
often been made by various interpreters of prophecy to
connect the Feast of Trumpets with the Rapture of the
Church because at that time we are told the Lord will

descend from heaven, ". . . with the trump of God," but the context here shows us that the Feast of Trumpets does not in any sense typify anything connected with the heavenly calling, but has to do with the ingathering of Israel to their earthly inheritance. With this agree the words of our Lord which we noticed in a previous study, where He declared that at His Second Coming He would send forth His angels with a sound of a trumpet and gather together His elect from the four quarters of the earth. This makes the meaning of the Feast of Trumpets crystal clear and shows its direct application to the regathering of Israel.

If the Feast of Trumpets had to do with the Rapture of the Church, there would be no place for that which follows in Leviticus 23 because immediately afterwards we have the second "set time" in this latter series for Israel — the great Day of Atonement, when Israel shall recognize in the Lord Jesus Christ the One who made atonement for their sins but whom up to that time they will not have known. Let us read carefully verses 26 through 32:

> "And the Lord spake unto Moses, saying, Also on the tenth day of this seventh month there shall be a day of atonement: it shall be an holy convocation unto you; and ye shall afflict your souls, and offer an offering made by fire unto the Lord. And ye shall do no work in that same day: for it is a day of atonement, to make an atonement for you before the Lord your God. For whatsoever soul it be that shall not be afflicted in that same day, he shall be cut off from among his people. And whatsoever soul

it be that doeth any work in that same day, the same
soul will I destroy from among his people. Ye shall
do no manner of work: it shall be a statute for ever
throughout your generations in all your dwellings.
It shall be unto you a sabbath of rest, and ye shall
afflict your souls: in the ninth day of the month at
even, from even unto even, shall ye celebrate your
sabbath" (Leviticus 23:26-32).

These verses can have no reference to the Church
as such for already we have seen set forth in the Passover the same truth which is now brought before us
here, but the great point of the type is that inasmuch
as Israel failed to apprehend the meaning of the Passover, it will not be until the coming day of tribulation
when they are in distress and sorrow that they will
realize the fact that the Saviour whom their fathers
rejected was the One who actually made atonement for
their sins. This great Day of Atonement as observed
by Israel in the latter day is set forth in Zechariah 12,
verses 10 to 14:

"And I will pour upon the house of David, and
upon the inhabitants of Jerusalem, the spirit of
grace and of supplications: and they shall look upon
me whom they have pierced, and they shall mourn
for him, as one mourneth for his only son, and shall
be in bitterness for him, as one that is in bitterness
for his firstborn. In that day shall there be a great
mourning in Jerusalem, as the mourning of Hadad-
rimmon in the valley of Megiddon. And the land
shall mourn, every family apart; the family of the
house of David apart, and their wives apart; the
family of the house of Nathan apart, and their wives
apart; the family of the house of Levi apart, and
their wives apart; the family of Shimei apart, and
their wives apart; all the families that remain, every
family apart, and their wives apart."

In that day when Israel shall realize how terribly they
have blundered in refusing the Lord Jesus Christ when
He came in lowly grace, they will bow before God in
bitterness of soul and confess their sin.   In the first
verse of chapter 13 we are told the result:

> "In that day there shall be a fountain opened to
> the house of David and to the inhabitants of Jeru-
> salem for sin and for uncleanness" (Zech. 13:1).

In other words, Israel's cleansing will come when in
spirit they reach the true Day of Atonement and recognize the once rejected Jesus as their Saviour and Lord.
Then they will cry, in the words of Isaiah 53, "He was
wounded for our transgressions, he was bruised for our
iniquities: the chastisement of our peace was upon him;
and with his stripes we are healed." That entire wonderful chapter will open up to them in a marvelous way
as the Holy Spirit reveals to them their sin and their
Saviour.

One feast remains ere the year is closed — the Feast
of Tabernacles or of Ingathering. This was for Israel
the happiest festival of all the year. It was the time
when they dwelt in booths as a reminder of the tents
of the wilderness and when they all rejoiced together
in the good things God had given them through the
vintage and the harvest. We have quoted before and
so it will be well to quote again here the actual instruction given in this chapter in Leviticus:

> "And the Lord spake unto Moses, saying, Speak
> unto the children of Israel, saying, The fifteenth day
> of this seventh month shall be the feast of taber-
> nacles for seven days unto the Lord. On the first day

shall be an holy convocation: ye shall do no servile work therein. Seven days ye shall offer an offering made by fire unto the Lord: on the eighth day shall be an holy convocation unto you; and ye shall offer an offering made by fire unto the Lord: it is a solemn assembly; and ye shall do no servile work therein. These are the feasts of the Lord, which ye shall proclaim to be holy convocations, to offer an offering made by fire unto the Lord, a burnt-offering, and a meat-offering, a sacrifice, and drink-offerings, every thing upon his day: beside the sabbaths of the Lord, and beside your gifts, and beside all your vows, and beside all your freewill-offerings, which ye give unto the Lord. Also in the fifteenth day of the seventh month, when ye have gathered in the fruit of the land, ye shall keep a feast unto the Lord seven days: on the first day shall be a sabbath, and on the eighth day shall be a sabbath. And ye shall take you on the first day the boughs of goodly trees, branches of palm trees, and the boughs of thick trees, and willows of the brook; and ye shall rejoice before the Lord your God seven days. And ye shall keep it a feast unto the Lord seven days in the year. It shall be a statute for ever in your generations: ye shall celebrate it in the seventh month. Ye shall dwell in booths seven days; all that are Israelites born shall dwell in booths: that your generations may know that I made the children of Israel to dwell in booths, when I brought them out of the land of Egypt: I am the Lord your God. And Moses declared unto the children of Israel the feasts of the Lord" (Leviticus 23:33-44).

Surely anyone familiar with the Word of God can see in this the picture of that wonderful day when the Lord Jesus shall return in power and glory, and His earthly people will be brought into blessing here in the world and will dwell beneath their own vine and fig tree, rejoicing in the goodness of the Lord. Then the

prophecy of Zechariah will have its perfect fulfillment.
The Feast of Tabernacles and the deliverance of the
people are identical. This is set forth clearly in Zechariah 14, verses 16 to 21:

> "And it shall come to pass, that every one that is
> left of all the nations which came against Jerusalem
> shall even go up from year to year to worship the
> King, the Lord of hosts, and to keep the feast of
> tabernacles. And it shall be, that whoso will not
> come up of all the families of the earth unto Jeru-
> salem to worship the King, the Lord of hosts, even
> upon them shall be no rain. And if the family of
> Egypt go not up, and come not, that have no rain;
> there shall be the plague, wherewith the Lord will
> smite the heathen that come not up to keep the feast
> of tabernacles. This shall be the punishment of
> Egypt, and the punishment of all nations that come
> not up to keep the feast of tabernacles. In that day
> shall there be upon the bells of the horses, HOLI-
> NESS UNTO THE LORD; and the pots in the
> Lord's house shall be like the bowls before the altar.
> Yea, every pot in Jerusalem and in Judah shall be
> holiness unto the Lord of hosts: and all they that
> sacrifice shall come and take of them, and seethe
> therein: and in that day there shall be no more the
> Canaanite in the house of the Lord of hosts."

And so the wonderful story comes to an end, and
Israel, for so long the nation of the wandering foot, will
at last have found their rest in subjection to and glad
recognition of the Lord Jesus Christ who was not recognized by them when He came to fulfill the type of the
Passover and the firstfruits, but who in that day will be
manifested to them as the One who made atonement for
their sins upon the cross and under whose righteous rule
they shall find rest after all the sorrows and trials they

have endured throughout the centuries since they cried, "Away with Him, away with Him; crucify Him, crucify Him."

The break between the two sets of feasts is clear and definite, and is corroborative evidence that our interpretation of the parenthesis in Daniel 9 is the very truth of God in regard to His prophetic dealings with Israel and the world.

Chapter VIII

THE MYSTERY OF THE OLIVE TREE

If my reader has followed me thus far, he will be prepared now to examine with a degree of intelligence the place that the Great Parenthesis occupies in what is itself a parenthesis — the great dispensational division of the Epistle to the Romans as set forth in chapters 9, 10 and 11. It is proper to speak of these chapters as a parenthesis because so far as the doctrinal unfolding of the truth of the righteousness of God as revealed in the Gospel is concerned, one could move on without being conscious that anything was missing between the closing verses of chapter 8 and the opening verses of chapter 12. In the first eight chapters of this epistle we have unfolded for us God's method of dealing with sin according to the righteous demands of His throne, and His Way of providing a perfect righteousness for men who have none of their own. Then in chapters 12 to 16 we see the effects of all this upon the life of the obedient believer: practical righteousness manifested in the lives of those who have been made the righteousness of God in Christ. But between chapters 8 and 12 we have a great parenthetic division in which the Apostle turns aside, as guided by the Holy Spirit, to show how the present proclamation of the Gospel of the grace of God harmonizes with God's former revelation to Israel and His electing grace in making them His covenant people.

In Romans 3 we learn that there is no difference, that all have sinned and come short of the glory of God. The Jew is shown to have no more claim upon the grace of God in Christ than the Gentile. All must come to God in exactly the same way, as needy sinners trusting His blessed Son for salvation. This would naturally raise the question in the mind of any honest Jew: But what then of the special promises made to Israel? What of the covenant entered into at Sinai? How does this affect the promise made to Abraham and to his seed? These questions and others of kindred character are answered fully and completely in chapters 9 to 11.

In chapter 9 the Spirit of God speaks particularly of the Lord's past dealings with Israel; in chapter 10, of His present dealings with them; and in chapter 11, of His future dealings, which will be in exact accord with the prophetic Word.

Turning, then, to chapter 9, we see that Israel was an elect nation. It pleased God to separate this people from all other peoples unto Himself in order that they might occupy a special place of testimony in the earth. This privilege was not given to them because of any merit of their own. It was in sovereign, electing grace that God chose Isaac and set Ishmael to one side, and again chose Jacob and set Esau to one side. God was not unrighteous in doing this. He was the Creator. Like the potter, He had power over the clay to make of it whatever He would. If any object to the truth of election in this sense, the answer to every objection is simply this: God has a right to do as He wills. He chose Israel and made that nation the depositary of His promises, and this was in order that they might be a means of blessing to the whole world.

It is a great mistake, however, to attempt to read eternal things into the ninth chapter of Romans. There is nothing in this chapter about election to eternal life or a place in heaven, and certainly nothing about repro- bation to eternal judgment in hell. When hyper-Calvin- ists attempt to use this portion of Scripture to support their God-dishonoring views, they wrest the Word from its true setting. It is election to a place of privilege on earth, not to eternal blessedness, and the rejection of which it speaks must be looked at in the same way, as having to do with earthly things and not with heavenly. God chose Abraham to be the father of the covenant people. In the next generation He declared: "In Isaac shall thy seed be called"; and in regard to the sons of Isaac it is written: "The children being not yet born, neither having done any good or evil, that the purpose of God according to election might stand, not of works, but of him that calleth; it was said unto her [that is, unto Rebekah], The elder shall serve the younger. As it is written, Jacob have I loved, but Esau have I hated" (Romans 9:11-13). Observe, it was not said: "The younger shall go to heaven and the elder shall go to hell." God was not speaking of eternal things at all, but the elder was set aside in favor of the younger so far as privilege on earth was concerned.

The thirteenth verse must be understood relatively. Compared with the blessing God gave to Jacob, it would seem as though He hated Esau, but we need to remember that this statement was not made before the children were born, but long years after in the book of Malachi, chapter 1, verses 2 and 3, where God is tracing out the history of His ways with the descendants of the two sons of Isaac, and He shows how privileged Jacob, or Israel, had been and how destitute of many similar blessings Esau, or Edom, had been.

Now if God thus chose to take up the seed of Abraham after the flesh and they failed completely as a nation to appreciate His goodness, and when His own Son came into the world they fulfilled their own Scriptures in condemning Him, who shall question the righteousness of God in setting them to one side and taking up the Gentiles and giving to them the glorious privileges that they now enjoy?

So, in chapter 10 we have, as already intimated, God's present dealings with Israel. He has set the nation as such to one side during all this long parenthetic period which we have been considering, but that does not mean that the individual Jew is left without an opportunity of salvation for eternity. Any Jew who will, may come to God in Christ and find salvation on exactly the same basis as any Gentile. So we read in verse 12: "There is no difference between the Jew and the Greek: for the same Lord over all is rich unto all that call upon him." And the apostle adds in verse 13: "For whosoever shall call upon the name of the Lord shall be saved." During all this present period, while Israel nationally is set to one side, God's "whosoever message" is going out to the world, and Jew or Gentile may avail themselves of it if they will, and if they refuse to do so, they are responsible for their own judgment.

In chapter 11 we have the future of this covenant people. We are told first that their eyes were blinded because they were so occupied with their own works that they rebelled against the grace of God. National Israel is judicially blinded to this present day, and this is in accordance with prophetic intimations, as we see in verses 7 to 12:

> "What then? Israel hath not obtained that which he seeketh for; but the election hath obtained it, and the rest were blinded (according as it is written, God hath given them the spirit of slumber, eyes that they should not see, and ears that they should not hear;) unto this day. And David saith, Let their table be made a snare, and a trap, and a stumbling-block, and a recompense unto them: let their eyes be darkened, that they may not see, and bow down their back alway. I say then, Have they stumbled that they should fall? God forbid; but rather through their fall salvation is come unto the Gentiles, for to provoke them to jealousy. Now if the fall of them be the riches of the world, and the diminishing of them the riches of the Gentiles; how much more their fullness?" (Romans 11:7-12).

God then has, if one may so say, taken advantage of the Jews' unbelief to open wide the door of grace to all men everywhere; and so the Gentiles are really indebted to the unbelieving Jews for their present wonderful opportunity. Surely it ill becomes any Gentile to look with contempt on or to speak in an unkind, derogatory way of the Jew because of his failure to understand God's plan when the Lord Jesus appeared on earth in accordance with the prophetic Scriptures! They did not understand, and so they lost a glorious opportunity, even as our Lord Himself said: "If thou hadst known, even thou, at least in this thy day, the things which belong unto thy peace! but now they are hid from thine eyes" (Luke 19:42). "Your house is left unto you desolate: and verily I say unto you, Ye shall not see me, until the time come when ye shall say, Blessed is he that cometh in the name of the Lord" (Luke 13:35).

And so with the setting aside of Israel, we have the Gospel of grace going out to the nations. Speaking from the standpoint of the Apostle of the Gentiles, Paul continues:

> "For if the casting away of them be the reconciling of the world, what shall the receiving of them be, but life from the dead? For if the firstfruit be holy, the lump is also holy: and if the root be holy, so are the branches. And if some of the branches be broken off, and thou, being a wild olive tree, wert graffed in among them, and with them partakest of the root and fatness of the olive tree; boast not against the branches. But if thou boast, thou bearest not the root, but the root thee. Thou wilt say then, The branches were broken off, that I might be graffed in. Well; because of unbelief they were broken off, and thou standest by faith. Be not highminded, but fear: for if God spared not the natural branches, take heed lest he also spare not thee. Behold therefore, the goodness and severity of God: on them which fell, severity; but toward thee, goodness, if thou continue in his goodness: otherwise thou also shalt be cut off. And they also, if they abide not still in unbelief, shall be graffed in: for God is able to graff them in again" (Romans 11:15-23).

The figure of the olive tree used here is taken from the book of Jeremiah, chapter 11 and verse 16:

"The Lord called thy name, A green olive tree, fair, and of goodly fruit: with the noise of a great tumult he hath kindled fire upon it, and the branches of it are broken."

There are three plants used in a special way as representing Israel. The *vine* speaks of them as God's testimony in the earth. The *fig tree* is the symbol of Israel nationally, and the *olive tree* tells of them as the covenant people in special relation to God. Because of their unfaithfulness and particularly their rejection of the Lord Jesus Christ, the natural branches were broken off from the olive tree of which Abraham is the root. He is the father of all that believe. Israel failed here, and so these branches were torn out of the tree of the covenant. In place of them, wild branches representing the Gentiles were grafted in, but we need to remember that these branches do not necessarily speak of individual souls actually saved, but of Gentile nations to whom privileges have now been granted which were heretofore uncovenanted so far as they were concerned. If there is real faith, they partake of the root and fatness of the olive tree. As we read in Galatians, "They that be of faith are blessed with faithful Abraham." But where the Gentiles manifest unbelief and heedlessness to the Word of God, they expose themselves to the same judgment that has already fallen upon Israel. The day will come when they will be torn out of the olive tree and their special privileges will come to an end.

Unbelieving critics have ridiculed the figure used here by the Apostle Paul, and have even taken occasion to point to it as a positive proof that the epistles are not definitely inspired by God. "How," they ask, "could God make such a mistake as that which Paul has made here? He speaks of grafting wild branches into a good tree, and every horticulturalist knows that you do not graft wild branches into a good tree, but you graft good branches into a wild tree in order to change completely the character of its fruit." But here, as elsewhere, it is the critics who are wrong. They do not read carefully enough, nor, shall I say, far enough. When we turn to verses 23 and 24, we read:

> "And they also, if they abide not still in unbelief, shall be graffed in: for God is able to graff them in again. For if thou wert cut out of the olive tree which is wild by nature, and wert graffed contrary to nature into a good olive tree: how much more shall these, which be the n a t u r a l branches, be graffed into their own olive tree?" (Romans 11:23-24).

Notice the expression, "If thou wert graffed contrary to nature into a good olive tree." Paul draws attention to the fact that the illustration he is using is not in accordance with ordinary custom, but is contrary to it, just as the matchless grace of God is contrary to the thoughts of man's legalistic heart. And if the Gentile nations have thus been so highly privileged, why should anyone wonder if, upon their failure, God should turn back again to Israel and graft in the natural branches into their own olive tree? This is exactly what He will do when the present period which we have described as the Great Parenthesis comes to an end.

And so we read in verse 25: "For I would not, brethren, that ye should be ignorant of this mystery, lest ye should be wise in your own conceits; that blindness in part is happened to Israel, until the fulness of the Gentiles be come in." We need to distinguish between "the times of the Gentiles" and "the fulness of the Gentiles." We have already seen that "the times of the Gentiles" covers the entire period during which the nation of the Jews, the city of Jerusalem, and the land of Palestine are under Gentile domination. This began with Nebuchadnezzar's conquest of Palestine and will end at the revelation of the Lord Jesus Christ from heaven at the close of the Great Tribulation, or as Daniel puts it, "the last end of the indignation." But the other term, "the fulness of the Gentiles," has to do with God's present work of grace. When He has taken out from among the Gentiles a people for His Name, when the last soul who is to be saved in this age has come to Christ, the Church will be completed and "the fulness of the Gentiles" will have come in. Then that Church will be caught up to be with the Lord before the seventieth week of Daniel begins. God will then take up Israel, and after the terrible time of tribulation spoken of specifically as "the time of Jacob's trouble," out of which Israel is to be saved, shall come to an end, the remainder of the nation will be brought into blessing. The apostate part of Israel will be destroyed as a result of the terrible experiences of the Great Tribulation. The remnant will be looked upon by God as the nation. And so says the Apostle in verse 26:

"And so all Israel shall be saved: as it is written, There shall come out of Zion the Deliverer, and shall turn away ungodliness from Jacob: for this is my covenant unto them, when I shall take away their sins. As concerning the gospel, they are enemies for your sakes: but as touching the election, they are beloved for the fathers' sakes. For the gifts and calling of God are without repentance. For as ye in times past have not believed God, yet have now obtained mercy through their unbelief: even so have these also now not believed, that through your mercy they also may obtain mercy. For God hath concluded them all in unbelief, that he might have mercy upon all. O the depth of the riches both of the wisdom and knowledge of God! how unsearchable are his judgments, and his ways past finding out! For who hath known the mind of the Lord? or who hath been his counsellor? Or who hath first given to him, and it shall be recompensed unto him again? For of him, and through him, and to him, are all things: to whom be glory for ever. Amen" (Romans 11:26-36).

Surely it is clear that these three chapters, then, fit in perfectly with what we have found elsewhere as to this parenthetic period between the sufferings of Christ and the glories that shall follow. The Old Testament reveals the truth that Israel would not recognize their Messiah when He came and that trouble and disaster would fall upon them because of this, but it gave no intimation of what God would do during this time of their setting aside in taking out a vast company of Gentiles to be associated with His Son throughout the Kingdom Age as His body and His bride. This is part of the great secret which had been kept in His heart from times eternal but now has been made known.

It may be well to point out what has been often noticed by others, that a "mystery" as spoken of in the New Testament is not necessarily something mysterious. It is a sacred secret which man could know nothing about until God revealed it. This mystery of the olive tree was made known only after the rejection of Christ and the consequent setting aside of the chosen nation.

What a day it will be when, God's present program completed, He will take up Israel once more and bring them at last to confess their sin and to look up in faith to the Saviour whom their fathers rejected, and confess Him as their Redeemer and their long waited for Messiah! Then Israel shall blossom and bud and fill the face of the whole earth with fruit, for they will become God's instruments for the enlightenment of the Gentile world.

Chapter IX

THE REVELATION OF THE ONE BODY

It is now time that we consider the particular ministry which God has committed to His Church, those whom He is taking out from both Jew and Gentile in this parenthetic period; and for this we must turn particularly to the letters of the Apostle Paul. Our Lord, before He left this scene, intimated to His disciples that He had come not only to seek the lost sheep of the house of Israel and to bring them out of the Jewish fold that they might be gathered to Himself, but He declared: "Other sheep I have which are not of this fold: them also I must bring, and there shall be one fold, and one shepherd." This as recorded in the tenth of John was perhaps the first inkling of one phase of the great mystery that during the present age Jew and Gentile were to be dealt with alike on the basis of pure grace, and all special distinctions had disappeared. "There shall be," said Jesus, "one flock." It took the disciples some time, however, to grasp the significance of this, and God had to give to the Apostle Peter a special revelation, as we have already seen, before he had faith enough to go to a Gentile household and proclaim the Gospel to them. But when he did so and they believed, the Holy Spirit fell upon them and they were united in happy fellowship with their believing brethren from among the Jews. This was in accord with the vision that Peter had seen and the word that came to him saying: "What God hath cleansed, that call not thou common."

Just prior to this, Saul of Tarsus had been converted on the Damascus road, and at the very moment of his conversion a revelation was made to him which was doubtless unfolded much more fully afterwards but which embodied the special truth which was given to him to make known to all nations for the obedience of faith. When the risen Lord asked the question, "Why persecutest thou me?" His words implied an intimate relationship between Christians and Himself which had never been previously emphasized. It was the revelation of the mystery of the one body in embryo. That question declared the wondrous fact that it is impossible to touch a child of God on earth without affecting the Lord Jesus Christ in heaven, for every believer is a member of His body, of His flesh, and of His bones.

In the Epistle to the Ephesians, Paul tells us that this was made known to him by divine revelation. Note his words as given in chapter 3:

"For this cause I, Paul, the prisoner of Jesus Christ for you Gentiles, if ye have heard of the dispensation of the grace of God which is given me to you-ward: how that by revelation he made known unto me the mystery; (as I wrote afore in few words, whereby, when ye read, ye may understand my knowledge in the mystery of Christ) which in other ages was not made known unto the sons of men, as it is now revealed unto his holy apostles and prophets by the Spirit; that the Gentiles should be fellowheirs, and of the same body, and partakers of his promise in Christ by the gospel: whereof I was made a minister, according to the gift of the grace of God given unto me by the effectual working of his power. Unto me,

who am less than the least of all saints, is this grace
given, that I should preach among the Gentiles the
unsearchable riches of Christ; and to make all men
see what is the fellowship of the mystery, which from
the beginning of the world hath been hid in God,
who created all things by Jesus Christ: to the intent
that now unto the principalities and powers in
heavenly places might be known by the church the
manifold wisdom of God, according to the eternal
purpose which he purposed in Christ Jesus our Lord:
in whom we have boldness and access with confidence
by the faith of him" (Ephesians 3:1-12).

Observe carefully what Paul here says. The truth he
was declaring was not made known by a study of the
Bible because it was not revealed in Old Testament
times. God waited until the parenthetic period had well
begun, which we have been considering in these passages. Then after there had been a final testimony to
Israel, calling upon any who realized their need of
Christ to acknowledge Him as Saviour and Lord, God
by revelation made known unto Paul this mystery or
secret which He had hidden in His heart from eternity.
It is called here in verse 4, "the mystery of Christ,"
and the term "Christ" as used here includes both the
Lord Himself and His redeemed people — He the Head
and they the members of His body, as we read in First
Corinthians 12:12:

"For as the body is one, and hath many members,
and all the members of that one body, being many,
are one body: so also is Christ.

The way by which we enter into this relationship is
given in the following verse:

"For by one Spirit are we all baptized into one
body, whether we be Jews or Gentiles, whether we be

> bond or free; and have been all made to drink into
> one Spirit."

Drinking suggests fellowship or communion. All who
are saved in this dispensation have been brought into
one blessed fellowship by the indwelling of the Holy
Spirit. It is the Lord Himself who baptizes into the
body, but the element, if I may so say, is the Spirit —
and not water. In water baptism we confess our personal faith in Christ. By baptism in the Holy Spirit the
Lord has made us members of His body. The earliest
members of the body, those who were baptized in the
Spirit on the Day of Pentecost, were all, of course, Jews,
but now Gentiles are made fellow-heirs, members of
the same body, and partakers of God's promise in Christ
by the Gospel.

This was not known, Paul tells us, in other ages, that
is, in the former dispensations; but it has now been
revealed unto Christ's holy apostles and prophets by
the Spirit. Notice that although it was to Paul primarily
that the revelation was given, he links up the other
apostles and New Testament prophets with himself as
recipients of this revelation. But in a very special sense
it was given to him to minister this truth to the people
of God. He speaks deprecatingly of himself as "the
least of all saints," doubtless remembering the time
when he persecuted the Church of God and wasted it;
but he rejoices in the fact that this special grace had
been given to him to preach among the Gentiles what
he calls "the unsearchable riches of Christ." This is the
Gospel (in all its fullness, and the end of it all is this:
"To make all men see what is the fellowship of the mys-

tery, which from the beginning of the world hath been hid in God, who created all things by Jesus Christ."

This expression "the fellowship of the mystery" is a very remarkable one. It tells us what real Christian fellowship is. We have communion one with another because we are members one of another. We have communion with the Lord because He is our Head and we are members of His body. All this is part of what our Authorized Version calls, "the eternal purpose of God." It might, perhaps, better be rendered "the purpose of the ages." Throughout all the ages God had this in mind, but He did not reveal it until the setting aside of Israel and the descent of the Holy Spirit to bring in the new dispensation.

In the Epistle to the Colossians Paul dwells on the twofold character of his ministry. He shows us there that he was a minister of the Gospel and also a minister of the truth of the mystery. In the first chapter he presents the Lord Jesus Christ as the first-born from the dead, the risen One who is now head of the body, the Church, in whom all the divine fullness is pleased to dwell. Then he adds:

"And having made peace through the blood of his cross, by him to reconcile all things unto himself; by him, I say, whether they be things in earth, or things in heaven. And you, that were sometime alienated and enemies in your mind by wicked works, yet now hath he reconciled in the body of his flesh through death, to present you holy and unblameable and unreproveable in his sight: if ye continue in the faith grounded and settled, and be not moved away from the hope of the gospel, which ye have heard, and

which was preached to every creature which is under
heaven; whereof I Paul am made a minister" (Colossians 1:20-23).

That which we could never do ourselves, He has done
for us. People speak sometimes of man's responsibility
to make his peace with God, but, alas, that he could
never do. It is impossible for sinful man to make atonement for his own iniquities, and until that is done, man
cannot be at peace with God. But the Lord Jesus has
made peace through the blood of His cross. On the
basis of this, the day will yet come when all things in
heaven and on earth will be reconciled to God. That
will occur when there will be a new heaven and a new
earth wherein dwelleth righteousness.

Observe that when it is a question of universal reconciliation we have only two spheres — heaven and earth.
In Philippians 2, verses 9 to 11, where God is dealing
with the question of subjugation rather than reconciliation, we have three spheres — heaven, earth and the
infernal regions. All will some day have to own the
authority of the once crucified Saviour, but not all will
be reconciled to Him.

Now those who have turned to God in repentance and
trusted Christ for themselves have already been reconciled to God through the death of His Son. Many, of
course, profess faith in Christ who by their after-lives
prove they are not genuine in their profession, but
where there is reality, this reconciliation is settled for
eternity. Of this glorious Gospel, Paul says he was
made a minister.

But now when we pass on to the last verses of the
chapter, we find he had a ministry to saints as well as
a ministry to sinners, and so he continues:

"Who now rejoice in my sufferings for you, and
fill up that which is behind of the afflictions of
Christ in my flesh for his body's sake, which is the
church: whereof I am made a minister, according to
the dispensation of God which is given to me for you,
to fulfil the word of God; even the mystery which
hath been hid from ages and from generations, but
now is made manifest to his saints: to whom God
would make known what is the riches of the glory of
this mystery among the Gentiles; which is Christ in
you, the hope of glory: whom we preach, warning
every man and teaching every man in all wisdom;
that we may present every man perfect in Christ
Jesus: whereunto I also labour, striving according to
his working, which worketh in me mightily" (Colossians 1:24-29).

This coincides with what we have already seen in the
Epistle to the Ephesians. It was given to Paul to fulfill
or complete the word of God by making known the mystery which had been hid from past ages, and generations
but which was now made manifest. It was Paul's earnest
desire to lead all of God's people into the truth of this
mystery. However, this does not mean for a moment that
some in the Early Church who had not yet received this
truth were not made members of the body of Christ,
even as it does not mean that thousands today who are
ignorant of it are thereby not included in the body. All
believers are members of the body, whether they know
the truth of it or not, but they have the greater joy as
they enter into and understand what God is now doing
and their special place of privilege and responsibility
in connection with it.

In closing the Epistle to the Romans after Paul had really completed the special unfolding of the Gospel and its blessed results in the lives of those who believe it, which was his particular object in writing this letter, he adds in an inspired postscript:

> "Now to him that is of power to stablish you according to my gospel, and the preaching of Jesus Christ, according to the revelation of the mystery, which was kept secret since the world began, but now is made manifest, and by the scriptures of the prophets, according to the commandment of the everlasting God, made known to all nations for the obedience of faith: to God only wise, be glory through Jesus Christ for ever. Amen." (Romans 16:25-27).

Notice again the expression used here, "the revelation of the mystery," which we are told, had been kept secret since the world began, or in all past ages. But it is now made manifest in prophetic writings. The expression translated in our Authorized Version "by the scriptures of the prophets" might imply that this mystery had now been discovered hidden in the books of the Old Testament prophets, but that is not what Paul wrote. He said: "It is now made manifest and by prophetic writings," that is, the prophetic writings of the apostles of the New Testament, "according to the commandment of the everlasting God, made known to all nations for the obedience of faith."

What a blessed thing it is to realize that this union of believers with Christ is something that once entered into can never be changed. It is unthinkable that the body of Christ should ever be dismembered or that anyone who was ever a member of His body should be lost at last.

Coming back again to the Epistle to the Ephesians, we find a very important exhortation in chapter 4, verses 1 to 7:

> "I therefore, the prisoner of the Lord, beseech you that ye walk worthy of the vocation wherewith ye are called, with all lowliness and meekness, with long-suffering, forbearing one another in love; endeavoring to keep the unity of the Spirit in the bond of peace. There is one body, and one Spirit, even as ye are called in one hope of your calling; one Lord, one faith, one baptism, one God and Father of all, who is above all, and through all, and in you all. But unto every one of us is given grace according to the measure of the gift of Christ."

We are called to walk worthy of our vocation, that is, the vocation or calling of members of Christ. We are to recognize a sevenfold unity. First we are told there is one body and one Spirit and one hope. The one Spirit here refers, of course, to the Holy Spirit in which we have been baptized into the body. The hope is that of the Coming of the Lord. Then we have another trio — one Lord, one faith, one baptism. The faith is that truth about Christ which we are called upon to confess. We acknowledge this in our baptism, thus owning the Lordship of Christ. We are no longer our own, but are to live as those who belong to Him. Then, finally, we have one God and Father of all, and He is above all and through all and in us all. This is the glorious truth of new creation. All believers are linked eternally with the risen Christ in glory.

So long as the body of Christ is on earth, it is our responsibility to make known the Gospel to the unsaved and the truth of this mystery to those who are already members of Christ. When the Church is taken out of this scene, God will no longer be dealing with the world in exactly the same way that He is now. There will be children of God in a coming age, but they will not be members of the Church which is Christ's body, the fullness of Him that filleth all in all. In the coming age the distinction between Jew and Gentile will be recognized once more. Restored Israel will be a priestly nation through whom the salvation of God will be made known to all the Gentiles, and they will be blessed in subjection to Israel as the special covenant people. The Church of this age will have its part with Christ in glory. When He reigns, we shall reign with Him as His body and His bride. How important, then, that we should appreciate our high and heavenly calling and seek now to glorify Him in all our ways, who has taken us into such intimate relationship with Himself.

The close of the Church's testimony on earth will come when the Lord Jesus returns for His own, before the dark days of tribulation begin. The Church must be out of this scene ere the seventieth week starts, and Israel will once more be recognized as God's covenant people. This involved another revelation which may be called "the mystery of the rapture." We read of it first of all in First Thessalonians 4, verses 13 to 18:

> "But I would not have you to be ignorant, brethren, concerning them which are asleep, that ye sorrow not, even as others which have no hope. For if we believe that Jesus died and rose again, even so them also which sleep in Jesus will God bring with him. For this we say unto you by the word of the Lord, that we which are alive and remain unto the coming of the

Lord shall not prevent them which are asleep. For the Lord himself shall descend from heaven with a shout, with the voice of the archangel, and with the trump of God: and the dead in Christ shall rise first: then we which are alive and remain shall be caught up together with them in the clouds, to meet the Lord in the air: and so shall we ever be with the Lord. Wherefore comfort one another with these words."

I speak of this as the first revelation of this particular truth because the Epistles to the Thessalonians were the earliest of Paul's letters which the Holy Spirit has preserved for the edification of the Church. There are other passages in preceding epistles, according to the order given in our English Bibles, which deal with this subject, but in point of time First Thessalonians gives the earliest written word in regard to it. Here we learn that when the Lord Jesus descends from heaven with a shout, He will call all His own to meet Him in the air. This is a very different thing from His Coming to the earth at the close of the Great Tribulation, when Israel will be in such distress, and He will appear in flaming fire, taking vengeance on their enemies, those who know not God. The two aspects of His Coming are altogether different. The Coming of First Thessalonians 4 is only for the saints. When He descends at the close of the tribulation period, He will come with His saints to execute judgment and to set up His glorious kingdom.

This special pre-Tribulation Rapture is not referred to in the Synoptic Gospels, and we have just a hint of it in John 14 where the Lord Jesus says: "If I go and prepare a place for you, I will come again, and receive you unto myself; that where I am, there ye may be also." Paul speaks of it as that which has come to him "by the word of the Lord." In other words, it was a special revelation made known in connection with the truth of the one body. In one of his later letters, First Corinthians, chapter 15, he gives us additional information in regard to this glorious event, and there he speaks of it very definitely as a mystery. He says:

> "Behold, I shew you a mystery; We shall not all sleep, but we shall all be changed, in a moment, in the twinkling of an eye, at the last trump: for the trumpet shall sound, and the dead shall be raised incorruptible, and we shall be changed. For this corruptible must put on incorruption, and this mortal must put on immortality. So when this corruptible shall have put on incorruption, and this mortal shall have put on immortality, then shall be brought to pass the saying that is written, Death is swallowed up in victory. O death, where is thy sting? O grave, where is thy victory? The sting of death is sin; and the strength of sin is the law. But thanks be to God, which giveth us the victory through our Lord Jesus Christ. Therefore, my beloved brethren, be ye stedfast, unmoveable, always abounding in the work of the Lord, forasmuch as ye know that your labour is not in vain in the Lord" (I Corinthians 15:51-58).

Observe that this aspect of His Return will take place at the sounding of the last trump. This is called in the Thessalonian passage "the trump of God," and it should be distinguished very definitely from the last of the seven angels' trumpets as mentioned in the book of Revelation, chapter 11. These angel trumpets will sound during the last half of Daniel's seventieth week, and the final trumpet ushers in the glorious kingdom of our Lord Jesus Christ. The trump of God is something altogether different. It is called "the last trump" because it will close the present age of grace and conclude God's ways with His people in this dispensation.

I have no doubt that those expositors are right who understand the expression "the last trump" to be an allusion to the third trump of the Roman legions. When the first trumpet sounded, whether it came in the night or in the day, the soldiers sprang to their feet and struck their tents. When the second trumpet sounded, they fell into line. At the last trumpet they marched away. And so we who believe have heard the first trumpet, awakening us when we were asleep in our sins. The second trumpet has called us to recognize the authority of our Lord Jesus Christ. Now we await the sounding of the last trump when we shall be caught away to be with Him forever. Then those who are living in their natural, mortal bodies will suddenly put on immortality. That is, the body will be changed in a moment, in the twinkling of an eye, and made like unto the glorious resurrection body of our Lord Jesus Christ. Those who have died and whose bodies have corrupted in the grave, will be raised to incorruptibility, and in their new bodies will be with and like Christ forever. This is our hope. For this we are called to wait. At any moment the Lord Jesus may return to fulfill these Scriptures. How blessed to be ready to hail Him with joy at His Advent!

Chapter X

THE MYSTERY OF LAWLESSNESS AND THE REVELATION OF THE MAN OF SIN

In his earliest epistle, the First Epistle to the Thessalonians, the Apostle Paul unfolded the precious truth of what we commonly call the "Rapture" of the Church. It is sometimes objected that the word "rapture" is not found in the Scriptures. This is perfectly true, but it does not therefore militate against the truth generally so designated. There are many other terms which are not actually found in the Bible and yet are themselves thoroughly Scriptural inasmuch as they are used to denominate doctrines which are clearly taught in the Word of God.

We do not find the word "trinity" in the Bible, but we do learn that God has revealed Himself in three Persons, the Father and the Son and the Holy Spirit, and this of course is the Holy Trinity. The word "substitution" is not found in Scripture, but when the Apostle exclaims, "The Son of God loved me, and gave himself for me," and when Isaiah declares, "He was wounded for our transgressions, he was bruised for our iniquities," both are teaching the great truth of substitution.

And so we need not be troubled because we do not find the actual word "rapture" either in Paul's writings or elsewhere in the New Testament, for to be raptured is to be caught away, and in this first letter to the Thessalonians, as well as in other passages, we learn that the Church of God will be caught away to be with the Lord at His Return to the air. This is what we mean when we speak of the Rapture.

In seeking to comfort some of the troubled Thessalonians who were grieving because they had lost friends in Christ by death, the Apostle told them of a special revelation he had received of the Lord which, as we have already noticed, is identical with that mystery made known later, in the fifteenth chapter of First Corinthians. This is the Coming of the Lord for His saints at the close of the present dispensation and prior to the beginning of the period of judgment which is to follow. Some have supposed that the Church would go into that time of trial and tribulation, but they forget that it is to be the time of Jacob's trouble, not that of the Church's testing.

There are also those who, because of present war conditions, insist that we are already in the tribulation and that the Church perhaps will be here for at least the first half of it, but will be caught up in the midst of the seventieth week, before the intense judgments are poured upon the earth; but they surely forget that the seventieth week begins with the signing of a covenant between the head of the ten-kingdom empire yet to arise and someone, evidently the Antichrist, representing the people of Israel. That covenant has not yet been signed. Therefore, we are not in the first half of the week. It will never be signed so long as God is still taking out from among the Gentiles a people to His Name. It will not be until He is once more recognized as in covenant relationship with Israel and the apostate part of the people make a "covenant with death and hell," as Isaiah calls it (Isaiah 28:18), that the seventieth week will begin.

This, however, was not clear to those early Thessalonian Christians, and when trial and persecution arose, they became perplexed and forgot the clear, definite teaching of the Apostle concerning the hope of the Lord's return to take His own to be with Himself ere the judgments began, and many wondered if they were not already entering the Great Tribulation with all its terrors. To them it seemed as though nothing could be worse than what they were already enduring, and the teaching was promulgated by some among them that the actual Day of the Lord was upon them — that great and dreadful day when He will deal in judgment with the nations of the world and His wrath will be poured out upon those who have rejected His Gospel. It is even possible, nay, actually probable, as one gathers from Second Thessalonians 2, verse 3, that someone had forged a letter, pretending it came from the Apostle Paul, declaring this very thing; and so bewildered saints were in confusion of mind and had lost sight of the blessed hope which had meant so much to them in the days of their first love.

To correct all this, Paul wrote his second letter. In the first chapter of that letter he speaks of the Coming of the Lord with all His saints when He appears in judgment. Surely no one who compares this passage with First Thessalonians 4:13-18 could ever dream of confounding them. In Second Thessalonians 1:7-10 we read:

"And to you who are troubled rest with us, when
the Lord Jesus shall be revealed from heaven with
his mighty angels, in flaming fire taking vengeance
on them that know not God, and that obey not the
gospel of our Lord Jesus Christ: who shall be pun-
ished with everlasting destruction from the presence
of the Lord, and from the glory of his power; when
he shall come to be glorified in his saints, and to be
admired in all them that believe (because our testimony among you was believed) in that day."

What a scene is this! And how different from the
peace and blessedness of the picture given of the descending Christ calling His own to Himself, as we have
it in the first epistle.   There, there is no flaming fire, no
taking vengeance upon the ungodly, but we see the
Bridegroom coming for His bride, the Head of the
Church calling all His members to be with Himself
before the judgments fall upon the earth.

In the second chapter of this second epistle Paul comes
directly to the point. Notice verses 1 and 2:

"Now we beseech you, brethren, by the coming of
our Lord Jesus Christ, and by our gathering together
unto him, that ye be not soon shaken in mind, or
be troubled, neither by spirit, nor by word, nor by
letter as from us, as that the day of Christ is at
hand" (II Thessalonians 2:1-2).

He bases everything that he is about to say upon the
truth he has already declared concerning the Coming
of our Lord Jesus Christ and our gathering together unto
Him. It is as though he were saying to these believers,
"I beg of you, brethren, in view of what I have already
made known to you concerning the precious truth of
that which is to be the consummation of all our hopes,
the coming of our Lord Jesus to the air, when the dead

will be raised and the living changed and we shall all be gathered together unto Him, that you do not allow yourselves to be misled or to be troubled in mind as though the present difficulties you are passing through and the persecutions you are called upon to endure indicate that the actual Day of the Lord is almost upon you."

Notice that whereas in the Authorized Version we read in verse 2, "the day of Christ," it is in every critical translation rendered, "the day of the Lord." This was what they feared. "The day of Christ" always refers to the time when the saints will be gathered around the Lord Jesus Christ in the air and we will stand before His judgment seat. That will be the Day of manifestation for believers only referred to so frequently in the epistles, but the Day of the Lord is the time when He will be manifested in judgment. It includes the pouring out of His wrath during the Great Tribulation and the entire Kingdom Age that will follow.

If someone professed to have a revelation by the Spirit or another declared that he had found in the Word (that is, the Word of God) that the Church was to go through the Great Tribulation, or if someone else presented a forged letter as though it came from Paul himself, he would not have the saints believe it. The Coming of the Lord Jesus Christ and our gathering together unto Him must occur first. The Great Tribulation cannot begin until the man of sin has been manifested, but that will never be so long as the Holy Spirit is here in the earth working in and through the Church.

This comes out clearly in the verses that follow. He says:

> "Let no man deceive you by any means: for that day shall not come, except there come a falling away first, and that man of sin be revealed, the son of perdition; who opposeth and exalteth himself above all that is called God, or that is worshipped; so that he as God sitteth in the temple of God, shewing himself that he is God. Remember ye not, that, when I was yet with you, I told you these things?" (II Thessalonians 2:3-5).

The expression "a falling away" might better be rendered "the apostasy." It refers not to such fallings away from the truth as have taken place again and again throughout the Christian dispensation, but the complete repudiation of Christianity and everything that is of God, when Babylon the Great, the false religious system of the last days, will hold sway over all Christendom, and the man of sin, the embodiment of all impiety, Satan's pretended Christ, will be manifested. He is called definitely, as Judas was, "the son of perdition."

We are not to suppose, as some have taught, that Satan will have the power of resurrection. It is only God who raises the dead. Therefore, this son of perdition is not identical with Judas as though he were to be brought forth from the tomb and become the Antichrist, but just as Satan entered into Judas and so controlled and dominated him that he sold the Christ of God, so Satan will enter into and dominate and control this blasphemous leader of Israel in the last days that he will set himself up to destroy everything of God on the earth. His description as given in verse 4 is almost identical with that of the willful king in Daniel 11. He opposes and exalts himself above all that is called God or that is worshiped. He takes his place in the Temple of God, a Temple doubtless to be rebuilt in Jerusalem in the end-times, and there declares himself to be divine.

Some have thought that the man of sin is to be identified with the first beast of Revelation 13, because we are told that all men shall worship him whose names are not written in the book of life of the slain Lamb. But the worship here mentioned is in the sense of doing homage, just as millions today do homage to Adolph Hitler and look upon him as an invincible leader against whom none can successfully fight. But the man of sin is a religious leader, not simply the head of a state, and is unquestionably, at least to my mind, identical with the second beast of Revelation 13, the one who will have two horns like a lamb, that is, who looks like the Lamb of God (therefore is the false messiah), but who speaks as a dragon, for he will be energized by Satan.

Paul tells the Thessalonians that when he was with them he had mentioned these things to them, and then he goes on to explain something that they had evidently forgotten.

> "And now ye know what withholdeth that he might be revealed in his time. For the mystery of iniquity doth already work: only he who now letteth will let, until he be taken out of the way. And then shall that Wicked be revealed, whom the Lord shall consume with the spirit of his mouth, and shall destroy with the brightness of his coming: even him, whose coming is after the working of Satan with all power and signs and lying wonders, and with all deceivableness

of unrighteousness in them that perish; because they
received not the love of the truth, that they might be
saved" (II Thessalonians 2:6-10).

Let us examine these verses carefully. "You know,"
the Apostle says, "what withholdeth," that is, what hinders, what restrains, what keeps back the full manifestation of iniquity — the revelation of the man of sin.
Paul had told them of a power that was already in the
world which kept evil from rising to its full height.
There has been much speculation as to what he meant
by this withholder or hinderer. Some have supposed
that he was speaking cryptically of the Roman Empire,
intimating its destruction, and declaring that the man
of sin could not be revealed until the Roman Empire
fell. Those who so teach generally think of the man of
sin as the Papacy. That the Papacy is anti-Christian
cannot be questioned by those who believe and know the
truth, but the man of sin is a definite individual, not a
system, who will arise at a given time and be destroyed
by Almighty power. Others have taught that the hinderer
is organized government, and this with a good deal more
plausibility. Their thought is that when the Church is
taken out of the world, all organized government will
collapse, and then out of the chaotic condition prevailing
among the nations, the man of sin will arise. But we
need to remember that the Apostle was inviting not only
for the Thessalonians in his day but for all believers to
the end of the dispensation, and when he says, "*Ye know
what hindereth* that he might be revealed in his time,"
he is speaking to all Christians.

Let me put the question directly to my reader. Do
you know what hinders or restrains the full manifesta-

tion of iniquity? I have asked this question over and over again of congregations, small and great, when Christian people were gathered together to study the prophetic Word, and always as with one voice the cry came back in answer, "Yes." And when I put a second question, "Who or what is the hinderer?" at once they replied, "The Holy Spirit." This seems to me so plain that I wonder that anyone could question it. In fact, the Prophet Isaiah declares this very definitely. In chapter 59, verse 19, he says: "When the enemy shall come in like a flood, the Spirit of the Lord shall lift up a standard against him"; or, as others have translated it, "The Spirit of the Lord shall resist him." He ever resists the powers of evil. As long as He is in the world doing His present work as the Spirit of grace, He resists the efforts of Satan to bring to the front his false Christ and to destroy God's testimony in this scene. And so we read that "the mystery of iniquity [or the secret of lawlessness] doth already work, only there is one now who hinders until he be taken out of the way [or out of the midst]."

The Lord Jesus said to His disciples, "When the Comforter is come, the Spirit of truth, He will abide with you forever." He, then, is here in the world working in and through the Church. As long, therefore, as the Church is in this scene, the Hinderer is here, holding back the evil; but Satan is working in a hidden way, duping men and women with false teachings and doing all he can to dishonor the name of the Lord Jesus Christ and to prepare them to receive the false Christ when he shall appear.

When the Holy Spirit, the Hinderer, goes up with the Church at the Rapture, then that wicked one, Satan's masterpiece, will be manifested, and for a time he will deceive the whole world, except the very elect (an election called out after the Church is gone), and even they will often be in perplexity and experience difficulty in standing against his persuasiveness. His doom, however, is certain. When the Lord descends in power and glory as indicated in the first chapter of this epistle, this evil personality will be destroyed by the brightness of His Coming.

But during the last half of the seventieth week he will deceive the nations by power and signs and lying wonders. Those who will be preserved in that day are designated in the prophets as "the remnant." This Jewish remnant will become God's messengers to the Gentiles who have not yet heard and resisted the truth, but for those who have heard and had every opportunity to be saved but persisted in refusing the message of grace, there is no possibility of salvation in that awful day. Because they refused the love of the truth when they might have known it, God shall send them strong delusion, that they should believe not merely *a* lie, but, according to the original text, *the* lie, that is, the lie of the Antichrist, that they all might be damned or doomed to judgment because they believed not the truth but had pleasure in unrighteousness.

That the believers of this dispensation will not be present on the earth in that day of Satan's power is clear from verses 13 and 14:

> "But we are bound to give thanks alway to God for you, brethren beloved of the Lord, because God hath from the beginning chosen you to Salvation through sanctification of the Spirit and belief of the truth: whereunto he called you by our gospel, to the obtaining of the glory of our Lord Jesus Christ" (II Thessalonians 2:13-14).

Caught away to be with the Lord before the judgments fall, the believers will be with Christ in the Father's house during the time of trouble here upon the earth.

And so it is evident that this revelation concerning the man of sin fits in perfectly with what we have been tracing throughout Scripture, the hidden purpose of God to call out His people during the parenthetic period between the sixty-ninth and seventieth weeks of Daniel's vision.

CHAPTER XI

THE END OF THE PARENTHESIS

We come now to consider the book of the Revelation. Within our present limits we can do this only in outline. I have taken it up more fully elsewhere.* My one thought now is to show how the bulk of the visions of the Apocalypse fit in after the Great Parenthesis has terminated.

The Lord Himself has indicated the divisions of the book of the Revelation in chapter 1, verse 19. We are told that He said to the Apostle John: "Write the things which thou hast seen, and the things which are, and the things which shall be hereafter." A somewhat more literal rendering of the last two parts of this verse would be: "The things which are now going on, and the things which shall be after these things."

At the time that the Lord uttered these words, John had only seen the vision of chapter 1, the Son of Man in the midst of the candlesticks. Therefore, we are justified in saying that the first division of this Book would be chapter 1, verses 1 to 18. The things which are now going on would embrace the next two chapters where, under the similitude of seven letters addressed to seven actual Christian churches or assemblies existing in the last decade of the first century of the Christian Era in the reign of the Emperor Domitian, under whose

*Lectures on the Book of Revelation by the same author can be obtained from the publishers.

tyrannical sway John was banished to the Isle of Patmos, we have an outline picture of the moral and spiritual conditions which the Lord saw would prevail through seven periods of the Church's history from apostolic days to the end of its testimony on earth. These churches were all located in the Roman proconsular province of Asia, where John himself, according to the best records that we have, spent something like the last thirty years of his life. For a very definite reason the Lord selected the particular seven that we have here. There were other cities in this province in which churches were located, but they are not referred to here. Hierapolis was one of them; Colossæ was another. The seven here selected will be seen, by consulting a map, to form a kind of a rough circle, so that if one took the highway from Ephesus, he would go on to Smyrna, then Pergamos, Thyatira, Sardis, Philadelphia and Laodicea, and from there back to Ephesus.

We are told in the twentieth verse of chapter 1, which introduces this division: "The mystery of the seven stars which thou sawest in my right hand, and the seven golden candlesticks. The seven stars are the angels of the seven churches: and the seven candlesticks which thou sawest are the seven churches." The Lord, then, is seen in the midst of these churches which are in the place of witness-bearing here on the earth. If we are only to think of the state and condition of the churches in the day when the Apocalypse was written, there is no particular mystery involved, but the mystery is now readily unfolded, for as we stand almost in the middle of the twentieth century, we can look back over all the years that have gone and see how remarkably these letters fit into seven great periods of Church history.

Observe, we do not have here specific historical facts as to individuals predicted. I mention this because some have objected to what has already been said because of the fact that the great outstanding characters of Church history seem to be utterly ignored. "How," one commentator asks, "could the letter to Sardis, for instance, speak of the great State churches of Protestantism when there is no mention of Luther, Calvin, or any of the other outstanding heroes of the Reformation?" The answer, of course, is that we are not dealing here with events or persons so much as with principles. In the letter to Sardis we see the moral and spiritual condition of Protestantism, and that is what the Spirit of God sought to make known. The most convincing proof that this suggested interpretation is the correct one is this: If we were to change the order of these letters in any degree, we would have confusion, but taken as they are, everything is in perfect accord with Church history. We cannot, for instance, substitute Sardis for Smyrna, Laodicea for Thyatira, Pergamos for Ephesus, or make any other change without spoiling God's wonderful portrayal of the prophetic story of the Church.

According to this view, then, we are now living in the Laodicean period of Church history. Ephesus sets forth the early days when living apostles still ministered to the Church on earth. Smyrna pictures the moral and spiritual conditions prevailing in the days of the ten great outstanding Roman persecutions. Pergamos tells of the union of Church and State in the days of Constantine and his successors. Thyatira is the Romish apostasy from the beginning of the seventh century, when the Pope first declared himself to be head of the Church on earth. It was then that the Papacy as such, with its amazing pretensions, really began. Sardis gives us, as intimated above, the great State churches of the Reformation with their uncounted thousands of baptized adherents who had a name to live but were dead. Philadelphia gives us the revival period, the second reformation when God's people were called back to the authority of His Word and the recognition of the all-sufficiency of the Name of the Lord Jesus Christ. Laodicea closes the series. It is the latitudinarian period of the Church, the era of modernism with its utter indifference to the truth of God and the claims of the Lord Jesus.

This, then, completes the series, and prepares us to consider the third division of the book, which John was told would have to do with the things which shall be after these things. When we open chapter 4 we read in the first verse, translated literally: "After these things I looked and, behold, a door was opened in heaven." From this point on we do not find the Church referred to again until, in the appendix to the book, in chapter 22, verse 16, we read: "I Jesus have sent mine angel to testify unto you these things in the churches. I am the root and the offspring of David, and the bright and morning star. And the Spirit and the bride say, Come." The bride is here identical with the Church and waits with longing heart for the Return of her Lord. But chapter 4 to the end of chapter 19 has to do entirely with events that will take place after the Great Parenthesis has come to an end.

While the seventieth week of Daniel may not begin immediately after the Rapture of the Church, we are not told of any lengthy period that will come in between that glorious event and the signing of the pact between the head of the revived Roman Empire and the Jewish people. In these stirring chapters we are occupied with events which will take place in heaven and upon earth during those last seven years, and it is very easy to see when the first three and one-half years will end and the last period, the forty-two months, or 1,260 days, of intense judgment, the Great Tribulation, begin.

In chapters 4 and 5 we see the heavenly saints in the glory with their Lord, worshiping before the throne, as represented by the twenty-four elders wearing victors' crowns upon their heads. No one wears a crown till after the Judgment Seat of Christ. Therefore, it is clear that these must represent the saints who will at that time have been raptured and who will have received their rewards at the hand of the glorified Saviour.

In chapter 6 we have the opening of the seals of the book of judgment which is also the title deed to this poor world. As the first six seals are opened, providential judgments fall upon this scene akin to those spoken of by our Lord Jesus as recorded in Matthew 24 which He designates, "the beginning of sorrows." In the book of Ezekiel, God speaks of His "four sore judgments" (Ezekiel 14:21). These refer not to his dealing with men in wrath but in chastisement, in order to bring them to repentance, if there be any disposition on their part to heed His voice. They agree perfectly with the seal judgments.

But in chapter 7 we have a parenthesis between the sixth and the seventh seals, and here we find 144,000 Israelites sealed before the Great Tribulation actually begins. The angel is instructed to "hurt not the earth, neither the sea, nor the trees, till we have sealed the servants of our God in their foreheads" (verse 3). In the latter part of the chapter we have a vision of a great multitude of Gentiles who will be saved in that day. They are pictured as they will appear when they have come through that awful time of trial, even as we read in verse 14: "These are they which came out of great tribulation [or more literally, the tribulation, the great one], and have washed their robes, and made them white in the blood of the Lamb." The Lord shows John these two groups that he may know that all the terrors of the Great Tribulation with the outpouring of the wrath of God in the earth will not hinder the Spirit of God from working from heaven upon the hearts of men and women who have not heard and rejected the Gospel in this parenthetic age but who will be still living on the earth in that day.

When the seventh seal is broken, seven angels are seen standing before God, to whom are given seven trumpets of judgment. The sounding of the first trumpet introduces the Great Tribulation; the sounding of the seventh trumpet brings it to an end and ushers in the glorious kingdom of our Lord Jesus Christ. We saw in the ninth chapter of Daniel that when the seventy weeks were finished, the vision of prophecy would be sealed up, and all would be complete. And in Revelation 10, verses 5 to 7, we read:

> "And the angel which I saw stand upon the sea and upon the earth lifted up his hand to heaven, and sware by him that liveth for ever and ever, who created heaven, and the things that therein are, and the earth, and the things that therein are, and the sea, and the things which are therein, that there should be time no longer: but in the days of the voice of the seventh angel, when he shall begin to sound, the mystery of God should be finished, as he hath declared to his servants the prophets."

The expression, "There should be time no longer," does not actually mean that eternity was about to begin, but "time" is used here in the sense of delay, as if one has an appointment at a certain hour and waits expectantly for another who has agreed to meet him, and finally, disappointed, says, "There is no more time," which simply means that he cannot longer delay. Note, then, that when the seventh trumpet sounds, the mystery of God's long toleration of evil will be ended. Everything will come out in the clear, and God's ways with men will be fully justified.

In chapter 11 we have further details as to this:

> "And the seventh angel sounded; and there were great voices in heaven, saying, The kingdoms of this world are become the kingdoms of our Lord, and of his Christ; and he shall reign for ever and ever. And the four and twenty elders, which sat before God on their seats, fell upon their faces, and worshipped God, saying, We give thee thanks, O Lord God Almighty, which art, and wast, and art to come; because thou hast taken to thee thy great power, and hast reigned. And the nations were angry, and thy wrath is come, and the time of the dead, that they

should be judged, and that thou shouldest give reward
unto thy servants the prophets, and to the saints, and
them that fear thy name, small and great; and shouldest destroy them which destroy the earth" (Revelation 11:15-18).

It is clear from this passage that the seventh trumpet
ends the Great Tribulation. It is not, as some have supposed, the same as "the trump of God" in First Thessalonians 4, otherwise called "the last trump" in First
Corinthians 15. In those passages the trump of God
sounds for the Rapture of the Church. Here the seventh
angel sounds his trumpet at the end of the tribulation
period to introduce the reign of Christ. It will be then
that all heaven will rejoice because the world-kingdom
of our God and His Christ will have come.

A second section of this third great division begins in
verse 19 of chapter 11, and goes on to the end of chapter
19, but with this we need not now be concerned. Those
who want to make a fuller study of it may do so at their
leisure, and there are many helpful books that would
assist the reverent student.

Chapter 20 gives us details as to the Millennial Kingdom, and we are carried on in the next two chapters to
the eternal kingdom. The book closes with an appendix
from chapter 22, verse 8, to the end.

There is one point that it may be well to dwell upon
inasmuch as many have been perplexed by it. Ordinarily
we speak of the Rapture as involving the first resurrection, but it is well to remember that the resurrection of
our Lord was part of that first resurrection and it also
includes the resurrection of saints who will be put to
death under the Beast and the Antichrist in the awful

days of the Great Tribulation. In chapter 20, after the
binding of Satan preliminary to the setting up of the
kingdom, we read, in verses 4 to 6:

> "And I saw thrones, and they sat upon them, and
> judgment was given unto them: and I saw the souls
> of them that were beheaded for the witness of Jesus,
> and for the word of God, and which had not wor-
> shipped the beast, neither his image, neither had re-
> ceived his mark upon their foreheads, or in their
> hands; and they lived and reigned with Christ a
> thousand years. But the rest of the dead lived not
> again until the thousand years were finished. This
> is the first resurrection. Blessed and holy is he that
> hath part in the first resurrection: on such the second
> death hath no power, but they shall be priests of God
> and of Christ, and shall reign with him a thousand
> years."

The question has often been asked, "If the first resurrection takes place at the close of the Great Tribulation,
how can it be said that the saints of this and past dispensations will be raised and living believers changed and
all caught up to heaven before the tribulation begins?"
In order to understand this clearly, let us examine the
passage carefully.

John says, "I saw thrones, and they sat upon them,
and judgment was given unto them." This has been
translated, "I saw thrones, and sitters upon them to whom
judgment was given." Now this is a distinct group, and
refers clearly to those symbolized by the twenty-four
elders who have already been before us in these marvelous visions of God. These are the saints of the Church
Age and of past dispensations. Then John indicates another class. He says: "And I saw the souls of them that
were beheaded for the witness of Jesus, and for the

word of God, and which had not worshiped the beast, neither his image, neither had received his mark upon their foreheads, or in their hands; and they lived and reigned with Christ a thousand years." The resurrection of this group completes the first resurrection. None others of the dead will live again until the Millennium is past. Speaking of both these groups, the Spirit of God says, "This is the first resurrection," and a blessing is declared as the portion of all who participate in it and who will be priests of God and of Christ and reign with him a thousand years.

With this Millennial Kingdom, human history on this earth will be concluded. When the wicked are raised at the end of the Kingdom Age and stand before the Great White Throne for judgment, the present created heavens and earth will be destroyed by fire from heaven and will be succeeded by that

> "One far off divine event,
>   Toward which the whole creation moves,"

when there shall be a new heaven and a new earth wherein dwelleth righteousness, where God will be all in all. This is the everlasting kingdom of our Lord and Saviour, Jesus Christ. It consists of two aspects — the heavenly and the earthly — but the new heavens and the new earth will be in such intimate relationship with the New Jerusalem descending from God out of heaven, linking both together, that it can be said when that eternal day begins, "God Himself shall be with them, they shall be His people, and He will be their God." Nothing will be permitted to disturb the happy relationship existing between God and His saints. The whole problem of good and evil will have been "threshed out," if I may use such a term, during the ages of time and those who are saved will be the exhibit of the grace of God through all the ages to come. Happy, surely, are those who shall have their portion with the redeemed in that glorious consummation!

PRINTED IN THE UNITED STATES OF AMERICA